Eyes
Remade
for Wonder

A
LAWRENCE KUSHNER
READER

INTRODUCTION BY THOMAS MOORE

For People of All Faiths, All Backgrounds

JEWISH LIGHTS PUBLISHING · WOODSTOCK, VERMONT

Eyes Remade for Wonder
A Lawrence Kushner Reader

Copyright © 1998 by Lawrence Kushner

Library of Congress Cataloging-in-Publication Data

Kushner, Lawrence, 1943-
Eyes remade for wonder : a Lawrence Kushner reader / by Lawrence Kushner ; introduction by Thomas Moore.
p.   cm.
Includes bibliographical references.
ISBN 1-58023-014-8 (hc).—ISBN 1-58023-042-3 (pbk.)
1. Spiritual life—Judaism. 2. Judaism—Essence, genius, nature.
I. Title.
BM723.K8676   1998
296.3—dc21   98-39081
                                                    CIP

First Edition: Simultaneous Paperback & Hardcover Release
ISBN 1-58023-014-8 (Hardcover)
ISBN 1-58023-042-3 (Paperback)

10 9 8 7 6 5 4 3 2 1

Manufactured in the United States of America

Jacket and interior design by Lawrence Kushner

For People of All Faiths, All Backgrounds
Published by Jewish Lights Publishing
A Division of LongHill Partners, Inc.
Sunset Farm Offices, Route 4
P.O. Box 237
Woodstock, Vermont 05091
Tel: (802) 457-4000 Fax: (802) 457-4004
www.jewishlights.com

for
the Members of Congregation Beth El
of the Sudbury River Valley

Table of Contents

Author's Preface

I REREAD THE OPENING PAGES OF MY FIRST BOOK, *The Book of Letters*, and it hit me: Everything I have ever written may be a commentary on this book's first chapter, which is about the letter *aleph*. This first letter of the Hebrew alphabet is almost, but not utterly, silent. "Open your mouth," I wrote in *The Book of Letters*, "and begin to make a sound. Stop. That is the sound of *aleph*."

That's what seekers of religious truth do. You devotedly, stubbornly, compulsively return again and again to that line between noise and silence, hoping against hope to find a way to say what finally cannot be said. If it could be said straight out, you wouldn't have to try to find a better way to say it. If you couldn't speak it at all, then you'd have to resort to such nonverbal modes of communication as art or dance or music. The thing about spiritual truth is that it wants to be spoken. It is too important, too transforming to be left alone in silence. It seems to have speakable content.

The problem is that once you speak or show the words to someone else, then both of you are different. The words have changed both of you. And now you must start all over again. I believe that in one form or another this making of words is the touchstone for all spiritual traditions and of all spiritual renewal: To say what is just at the outermost edge of what can be spoken is to deal with words that are so primary and dazzling that they are infinitely personal and intimate. And just that may be why we have religion. As I wrote in 1991 in *God Was in This Place and I, i Did Not Know*:

"Sooner or later we all lose that childlike ability simply to live each moment without reflection. We ask ourselves the great question. Overwhelmed by the mystery of existence, we are embarrassed to hear ourselves whisper, 'Who?' The question comes in many disguises and according to many timetables. For some, it takes shape only over decades. For others, the world is shattered in an instant. But sooner or later the question comes to every human being."

The Zohar, the master text of Jewish mysticism, says that everything God told us at Mount Sinai—which by definition would be everything that's worth knowing—is all contained in the *aleph*, the letter hovering just between speaking and silence. It seems to me now that the *aleph* may be more than the first letter of the *aleph-beit*. It may also be the last one too.

Laying out the selections of this book turned out to be something of a challenge. No two of my books are uniform in graphic presentation, content, or intended audience. (A colleague, Rabbi Ed Feld, once quipped that I seem to be compelled to invent a new literary genre for each book.) Some, like *The River of Light*, are more academic and have more extensive footnotes. Others, like *The Book of Letters* or *The Book of Words*, rely heavily on graphics as much as content for their teaching. *Invisible Lines of Connection* is all stories. *The Book of Miracles* was written (and illustrated) for children. *Honey from the Rock* and *God Was in This Place and I, i Did Not Know* are mystical theology (each with their own quirky footnoting apparatus). Some are written for a particularly Jewish audience, others for people of all faiths. The trick in compiling this anthology was preserving the format of the original material while also making this book a seamless read.

One further note on the notes. For the sake of consistency, all biblical, midrashic, and talmudic citations are now set within parentheses and embedded in the text itself. All the rest are set as endnotes.

Arthur Magida, my editor, and Jon Sweeney at Jewish Lights Publishing helped me choose the selections from my books, articles, and previously unpublished material that they especially liked and thought were representative of my work. They then guided me in arranging them. Generally each section moves from easy and introductory material such as *The Book of Letters* or *The Book of Miracles* on to longer and more complex selections.

The book begins with a section on awareness and then moves on to the touchstone for Jewish spirituality: sacred text. Section three addresses the struggle to be a human being. Section four is more mystical and considers how *everything* is a manifestation of God. The fifth section tries to integrate the implications of all this into communal and political action. Six is all about the mystic nothingness of God. And the last section, if I'm successful, returns us finally to our daily lives with a renewed gratitude for and an ability to simply be present wherever we are.

I had a professor at rabbinic school who used to say that most of us have only three or four sermons we work on refining and polishing over the courses of our lives. As I review all this, I am humbled to realize how accurate he was and only hope that the reader of this "reader" will find at least three decent teachings.

I want to thank Arthur Magida for his good-natured patience, wisdom, and sharp eye; my assistant, Elsie Navisky, for diligently transcribing so many of my pre-computer writings into electronic media; Bronwen Battaglia for her good graphic advice; Jennifer Goneau for her attention to detail; Larry Shuman for his creative devotion and unflagging energy; and Stuart Matlins and Jon Sweeney, publisher and vice-president respectively, of Jewish Lights, whose vision and support are responsible for this book. I am especially grateful to Thomas Moore for graciously consenting to write such an instructive and generous introduction. And, of course, my life-partner, Karen, restores my soul each day.

Introduction by Thomas Moore

As I approach my sixtieth year, I think solemnly and anxiously about the state of the world. I have a daughter full of vitality and promise and a stepson gifted beyond my understanding. As the years have gone by, I have lost most of my own Pollyanna idealism in relation to life, and I find myself worrying about the earth, my country, and the world that may or may not allow my children to fulfill the unlimited potential I see in them now. I feel frustrated by the self-serving materialism that dominates modern culture as it spreads to only recently converted nations, and by politicians and business leaders who ignore the most basic of human needs and seem blind to their murderous impact upon a fragile planet.

It is bad enough to live in a world powerful enough to destroy itself by means of its own heartless achievements and lack of insight; it is worse to see institutions of wisdom—the religions, the schools, and the helping professions—fall victim to the spirit of the times, forsaking wisdom for empirical smartness and confusing their own survival as institutions for service. Both those who need help and those who give it have given themselves over to the materialistic, narcissistic, and literalistic attitudes of the time.

Many look at the apparent renaissance of spiritual concern rising almost predictably at the end of the millennium and find strong hope. "There is a birth of spirituality," they tell me. These people, including some spiritual leaders, criticize me for my skepticism, calling me a cynic, accusing me of focusing too much on the dark side (as they put it) of human experience. But I don't feel comfortable in much of the new spirituality I see. It often feels gimmicky, ungrounded, and self-centered. It often sounds like self-improvement directed toward the spirit, and its aim appears to be success on the part of the enlightened one rather than service to a world in need of compassionate care.

Yet, in the midst of this classic, mid-life depressive view of the world, I have not lost my humor and my hope. I find much wisdom and dedication in the people I meet as I travel for book promotions and lectures. I find isolated people strategically countering their materialistic context and doing work that contributes both to their own need for meaning and to the welfare of those around them. I find artists creating beautiful buildings, intriguing paintings, and transporting music. A James Hillman in psychology, an Arvo Part in music, and a Toni Morrison in literature remind me that in the worst of times, genius and compassion may arise with gifts of extraordinary wisdom and beauty.

It is in this worried state—complicated with a sliver of hope, buttressed by an inherited spirit of fundamental optimism, and softened by an appreciation for the beautiful and the absurd—that I celebrate the achievement of Rabbi Lawrence Kushner. His writings have all the wisdom, the beauty, and the humor that often fail in modern culture and are completely absent from current religious and spiritual writing.

The first thing you may notice as you begin reading the following pages is the way Rabbi Kushner remains in close dialogue with his tradition. He is not making up a spiritual philosophy as he goes along; he is continuing an ancient tradition of reflecting on sacred texts and revered commentaries of those holy writings. His respect for received tradition removes his work from the personalism that is so characteristic of our times, grounding his words and giving them extraordinary weight and substance.

You will also notice the care with which he presents the traditional stories and his own thoughtful reflections. If you turn to the original sources from which these pieces come, you will find beautiful books. He takes care to make a book more than a channel for a heartless modern approach of communication, and instead makes a book an object of beauty and reverence. As a writer, I know how much attention and constant vigilance it takes to create a beautiful book in an age when it is acceptable to make a publication just passable. In this alone, in his attention to the book as a holy object, Rabbi Kushner is true to his tradition and is set apart from the pragmatic spirit of the times.

Another characteristic you will notice in the opening pages and throughout the book is a profound appreciation for narrative. Again, we live in an age charmed by empirical studies and cold concepts, but there is little wisdom, if any, in that style that is based more in the anxiety about being correct than in the comfortable enjoyment of insight. Rabbi Kushner tells wonderful stories, both from his tradition and from his experience; stories that stick in your memory and continue to offer insight like a time-release medicine capsule.

In this respect, there is something post-modern about Rabbi Kushner's work. He doesn't insist on the facts or the truth in any superior way, but instead he seduces the reader with stories that initially charm and then reveal an interior that is not as quaint as first appears. There is a studied intelligence in the selection, the telling, the placement, and the comment relating to these stories. The subtle use of narrative is a key element in distinguishing the genuine spiritual guide from the one who is merely compelled and caught by an idea. The former is the only guide worthy of our trust.

Many readers identify me with the soul, in spite of the fact that my sources and colleagues have written brilliantly about the subject. Rabbi Kushner doesn't write explicitly about the soul, yet he embodies in his writings all the characteristics of soul that one finds in traditional literature. He paints a sparkling picture of that vital realm that lies midway between the material and the spiritual, where ordinary days, family life, children, religious piety and symbol, and good humor lie; this is the realm I find traditionally described as the land of the meditating and humanizing soul.

Maybe this is why Rabbi Kushner invited me to write the introduction to this compilation of his life's work. I feel honored by the invitation. After all, I am a Catholic—even if my views depart from current official lines. In the mere act of asking me to write this introduction, I detect in Rabbi Kushner yet another quality of soulfulness and humanity: the capacity to transcend our ideological boundaries and to recognize our deeper brotherhood.

I find this brotherhood most convincingly presented in Rabbi Kushner's generous and unpretentious telling of the stories of his own life and his family. The vulnerability in telling stories honestly and simply, along with the recognition that family is the very heart of religion, spirits this wonderful collection of writings far away from the plethora of spiritual advice-giving and ideological advocacy that are such a prominent part of current spiritual literature. It gives added grounding. I have long stood in awe of the unfathomable wisdom in Judaism to honor its long chain of narrative and commentary and its awareness that religion, pure and simple, takes place most fully within the family.

Finally, the most telling sign of the presence of the human soul is humor. Not cynical, sarcastic, negative, and destructive wit, but the humor that grows from intimate familiarity with the very roots of life. Rabbi Kushner is never deadeningly serious. The comic joy of vitality lies ever close to the surface, if not at the very top of his storytelling. I trust the divine comic sense that gives life to these pages. Make no mistake: we are in the presence of a genuine spiritual guide.

One more footnote of a thought: Some anthologies and readers are mere patchworks of previously published work. This book is an original in its own right. It is put together with care. It is a new thing. It has its own identity and its own source of life. If you live your life the way this book is made, you will have all the heart, soul, and religion you need to live your individuality and humanity to the fullest and to turn this world in a different direction.

Rabbi Kushner ends his book with a blessing. I end my introduction with a word of thanksgiving for his talent in life and in literature.

Amazing Grace

RABBI YEHUDA ARYEH LEIB OF GER, author of one of the great works of Eastern European mystical theology, the *Sefas Emes*, commented that when Jacob dreamed about a ladder joining heaven and earth, he had attained a level of spiritual awareness that would have filled most people with pride. God had spoken to him personally and assured him of a successful future. Instead, however, Jacob was overcome with reverence.

"And Jacob awoke from his sleep.... Shaken, he said, 'How awesome is this place!'" To our surprise however, Jacob's ego does not get bigger, it gets smaller! Such reverence, says the Gerer Rebbe, is a sure sign that someone is on to great truth. Indeed, every event that occasions reverence also participates in ultimate truth. "Reverence is the beginning and the end of everything."

It happens to us too. Maybe we don't get the big dream or the personal speech but, like Jacob, we awaken to the mystery of our own existence and are overwhelmed with reverence. I'd call it "amazing grace." Just this is the beginning of all spiritual awareness: Reverence before The Mystery.

I have a friend who is a recent grandmother. Even though her granddaughter lives several hours away, she jumps at any excuse to spend time with her. Sometimes, if she is lucky, she even gets to baby-sit. On one such summer afternoon she was reading while the little girl played on the floor. Suddenly there was a clap of thunder and a torrent of rain. Within five minutes, she told me, it was over and the sun was shining again. The four-year-old wandered over to the window and exclaimed, "Grandma, who made that?" When my friend got up and looked outside she saw a complete rainbow.

The Kabbalists say that the ultimate question a human being can ask is not "what?" or "how?" or even "why?" The ultimate question is "Who?"

The Letter Aleph

ALEPH IS THE FIRST LETTER. IT HAS NO SOUND. Only the sound you make when you begin to make every sound. Open your mouth and begin to make a sound. Stop! That is *Aleph.*

It is the letter beginning the first of God's mysterious seventy names: *Elohim.* God. It also begins the most important thing about God: *echad.* One. Know that God is One. The first and the last and the only One.

The name of the first man was *Adam.* Adam. The first man. And the name of the herald of the last man will be *Eliyahu,* Elijah.

The name of the first Jew is also *Aleph, Avraham Avinu,* Abraham, our Father.

Aleph is the letter of fire, *aysh.* A fire that flames but does not destroy. That is how the Holy One gets your attention. God shows you the primordial fire.

And the very first letter of the first word of the first commandment begins with the first letter, which has no sound: *Aleph, anochi,* I. "I am the Lord your God who brought you out of the land of Egypt, the house of slavery."

It is no accident that all these words begin with *Aleph.* The most basic words there are begin with the most primal sound there is. The almost sound you make before you can make any sound.

Blessing as Awakening

BLESSINGS GIVE REVERENT AND ROUTINE VOICE to our conviction that life is good, one blessing after another. Even, and especially, when life is cold and dark. Indeed to offer blessings at such times may be our only deliverance.

We have specific and unique phrases by which we bless a sacred book before we read it, our children at the Sabbath table, our hands while washing them, the bread we eat, the moon, the fact that we are not slaves, and that the rooster can distinguish between night and day. We bless dwarfs and trees in first blossom. We bless the hearing of good news and any kind of wine. We bless everything. Or, to be technically correct, we bless the Holy One who stands behind and within them all.

Blessings keep our awareness of life's holy potential ever present. They awaken us to our own lives. Every blessing says, "I am grateful to be a creature and to remind myself and God that life is good."

With each blessing uttered we extend the boundaries of the sacred and ritualize our love of life. One hundred times a day. Everywhere we turn, everything we touch, everyone we see. The blessing can be whispered. No one even needs to hear. No one but the Holy One. "Holy One of Blessing, your Presence fills the universe. Your Presence fills me."

ORIGINALLY PUBLISHED IN *GENESIS II*, BOSTON, 1986

A Glistening Thread

"THERE IS NOTHING BESIDES THE PRESENCE OF GOD; being itself is derived from God and the presence of the Creator remains in each created thing."—Rabbi Menachem Nahum of Chernobyl[1]

The first chapter of Genesis is so familiar that we can easily overlook the obvious. I'll give you an example. Imagine there is an artist. There are rumors about his creativity. It is said that not only does he possess enormous energy but his artistic skills encompass many widely differing forms of expression. Imagine also that after years of curiosity, you have at last been invited to tour his workshop.

He holds up a piece of sculpture and says, "I made this."

It is very beautiful; you are impressed. Then, over on an easel, there is a freshly done canvas. "I made this too."

So he is not only a sculptor but a painter also. "And this bench here, I made it." A carpenter, he is. "And this electric drill, I made it also." So he is a machinist too.

"And the soufflé, would you like some? I baked it." He is also a gourmet cook. "And the window here; I made the glass. And this book; I wrote it. Bound it myself. Even made the paper. The music playing on the phonograph; it's mine." On and on it goes, until it seems that there is nothing in the entire workshop that the artist has not himself made.

What would you think? Well, first of all, it is obvious that we are in the presence of enormous talent. This artist made everything. But also we suspect that since all these creations are the work of a single artist they must share some common aesthetic motif or stylistic thread. And that it is only because of our relative inexperience in dealing with an artist of such enormous capability that we cannot discern the common hand in them all.

We remember once how in an art appreciation course in college we suddenly saw that the sculpture and the painting of Michaelangelo bore unmistakable common traits that any trained eye could see at a glance. Or perhaps we recall how after studying Beethoven, that the symphonies and the string quartets were clearly the work of the same genius. And that it had only been on account of our previous lack of sensitivity in such matters that made them initially sound dissimilar.

But now we are confronted with too much. We cannot go from the soufflé to the electric drill. They seem to have absolutely nothing in common, even though one and the same artist has made them. We know that they must be related to one another in precisely the same way that the painting and the sculpture or the symphony and the string quartet are related; they share a common maker. They are artistic siblings, each unique and yet each intimately related, each traceable to a common source.

It is that way with our world too. The apparent brokenness, disharmony, and confusion that clutter the universe are illusory. For everything in the world was fashioned by the same Artist. And this is perhaps why the author of the first chapter of Genesis is so intent on punctuating each day's work with the refrain, "And God made this and God made that". Which is to teach that everything is related to everything else and that if we would but look carefully enough, we could discern the work of the One Creator.

As Menachem Nahum suggested, "...the presence of the Creator can be found in all creation." One great glistening thread joining all being.

Awareness

THERE IS AN OLD HASIDIC STORY, recounted by Martin Buber, of the disciples who gathered to learn from their rebbe, the Baal Shem Tov, the founder of Hasidism. After the evening prayers, the master would go to his room where candles would be lit and "the mysterious Book of Creation" lay open on the table. All those seeking advice from the Baal Shem were then admitted in a group to hear their teacher, who would speak late into the night.

One evening as the students left the room, one apologized to the others for monopolizing so much of the Baal Shem's attention. Throughout the entire audience, the master had spoken to him personally. His friend told him not to talk such nonsense. They had all entered the room together and, from the very beginning, the master had spoken only to him. A third, hearing this, laughed and said that they both were mistaken, for their teacher had carried on an intimate conversation with him alone for the entire evening. A fourth and a fifth made the same claim, that the Baal Shem had spoken to them personally, to the exclusion of everyone else. Only then did they realize what had happened and all fell silent.[2]

So it is with us when we read scripture. The biblical text speaks intimately and demands an intensely personal response. As Harold Bloom has said of reading "strong poetry," the interpretation evoked "insist[s] upon itself...it and the text are one."[3] Because the words of the poem speak only to me, I am not free to comment dispassionately on them, for I am in them. They are me. What you say of the poem, you say of me.

There is a similar intensity of attention when Moses encounters God at the bush.

> Moses was tending the flock…beyond the wilderness and he came to the mountain of God, Horeb. An angel of the Lord appeared to him in the heart of a flame from inside a bush. And he looked and behold the bush burned in fire yet the bush was not consumed. Moses said, "I must turn aside now so that I can see this awesome sight: Why is the bush not consumed?" When the Lord saw that he had turned aside to look, God called to him from within the bush. (Exodus 3:1–4)

The story is customarily offered as a "miracle" that God performed to get Moses' attention. This fails to explain why God, who could split the sea, fashion pillars of fire, and make the sun stand still would resort to something so trivial and undramatic as to make a bush burn without being consumed to attract Moses' attention. It is a cheap trick.

Look more closely at the process of combustion. How long would you have to watch wood burn before you could know whether or not it actually was being consumed? Even dry kindling wood is not burned up for several minutes. This then would mean that Moses would have had to closely watch the "amazing sight" for several minutes before he could possibly know there even was a miracle to watch! (The producers of television commercials, who have a lot invested in knowing the span of human visual attention, seem to agree that one minute is our outer limit.)

The "burning bush" was not a miracle. It was a test. God wanted to find out whether or not Moses could pay attention to something for more than a few minutes. When Moses did, God spoke. The trick is to pay attention to what is going on around you long enough to behold the miracle without falling asleep. There is another world, right here within this one, whenever we pay attention.

The beginning of knowing about God is simply paying attention, being fully present where you are, or waking up. We realize that we have been asleep. We do not see what is happening all around us. For most of us, most of the time, the lights are on but nobody's home.

Right now, for instance, you are a reader. You are consuming these words and the ideas they bear. But suppose you were a typographer, then you would also notice the shapes of the letters. Suppose you were a poet. A paper manufacturer. A blind person. A composer. We find what we seek. And we seek who we are.

OBLIVIOUS TO MIRACLES

Jewish tradition says that the splitting of the Red Sea was the greatest miracle ever performed. It was so extraordinary that on that day even a common servant beheld more than all the miracles beheld by Isaiah, Jeremiah, and Ezekiel combined. And yet we have one midrash that mentions two Israelites, Reuven and Shimon, who had a different experience.

Apparently the bottom of the sea, though safe to walk on, was not completely dry but a little muddy, like a beach at low tide. Reuven stepped into it and curled his lip. "What is this muck?"

Shimon scowled, "There's mud all over the place!"

"This is just like the slime pits of Egypt!" replied Reuven.

"What's the difference?" complained Shimon. "Mud here, mud there; it's all the same."

And so it went for the two of them, grumbling all the way across the bottom of the sea. And, because they never once looked up, they never understood why on the distant shore, everyone else was

A LAWRENCE KUSHNER READER / 11

singing songs of praise. For Reuven and Shimon the miracle never happened. (*Shemot Rabba* 24.1)

Call it the difference between epistemology and piety. In epistemology if a tree falls in the forest and no one is there to hear, it may or may not make a sound. In piety if a miracle happens and no one notices, it did not happen. Each miracle requires at least one person to experience the miracle, even if, like Jacob, only in retrospect.

Now Jacob begins to ponder the events of his life in a new way. A dimension of what has come to be called "the spiritual" now lies open. "If God was here, and I didn't know, then perhaps God has been other places also."

JEWISH SPIRITUALITY

Classical Hebrew has no word for "spirituality." (The modern Hebrew, *ruchaniyut*, for "spirituality" comes from our English word.) The English word "spiritual" means immaterial and connotes the religious. The concept comes to us with the heavy baggage of early Christianity that divides the universe into material and spiritual. This tradition teaches how to leave this gross, material world and get to the other real, spiritual, and therefore holy one.

Judaism sees only one world, which is material and spiritual at the same time. The material world is always potentially spiritual. For Judaism everything, including, and especially, such apparently non-spiritual and grossly material things as garbage, sweat, dirt, and bushes, are not impediments to but dimensions of spirituality. To paraphrase the Psalmist, "The whole world is full of God." (Psalm 24:1) The business of religion is to keep that awesome truth ever before us.

Spirituality is that dimension of living in which we are aware of God's presence. "It is being concerned with," in the words of Martin Strelser, "how what we do affects God and how what God does affects us." It is an ever-present possibility for each individual.

Jewish spirituality is about the immediacy of God's presence every-where. It is about patience and paying attention, about seeing, feeling, and hearing things that only a moment ago were inaccessible.

INAUDIBLE SCREAMS

I once knew a man who was in psychoanalysis. His doctor's office was across the street from an old red brick, inner city psychiatric hospital. One day, as he had regularly done for a few years, my friend walked down the street to his car in front of the hospital when he heard a blood-chilling scream from the top floor that seemed to sound the deepest pain a soul could possibly feel. This unforget-table noise etched itself into his soul. The following day, back on the couch, he told his doctor of the scream from the top floor. To his astonishment, his therapist was surprised that he should men-tion it at all.

"You mean you just now heard it?" asked the doctor. "After all these years? On the top floor across the street, that's where they put all the screamers." And from that day on, my friend said, he was able to hear the screams on the top floor almost every time. "The screams are all around us," he later mused, "waiting for our ears and eyes and hands."

ULTIMATE AWARENESS

Aldous Huxley, paraphrasing Henri Bergson, once suggested that we are potentially able to be aware of everything.

> Each person is at each moment capable of remem-bering all that has ever happened to him and of perceiving everything that is happening everywhere in the universe. The function of the brain and nervous system is to protect us from being overwhelmed and confused by this mass of largely useless and irrelevant knowledge, by shutting out most of what we should otherwise perceive or remember

at any moment, and leaving only that very small and special selection which is likely to be practically useful.[4]

Universal consciousness is too much to handle and would burn out the circuitry. In Thoreau's words, "I have never yet met a man who was quite awake. How could I have looked him in the face?"[5] We must therefore create an elaborate system of filters, lenses, and blinders to screen out the extraneous images, leaving us with a very small field of vision. What we call consciousness is all that remains visible in this tiny patch of the light of our attention. We can aim it at anything we like, but only a very few things at a time. How we will focus and direct the beam is up to us.

BACKGROUND MUZAK

Eliyahu KiTov, the Orthodox Israeli commentator, poses this problem in classic religious terms.[6] We know that the Torah was given once and for all time at Sinai. Yet the Torah's words are so important that our sages say, "Each and every day the Divine Voice issues from Sinai." (*Avot* 6:2)

Not only then is Torah eternally unchanging, it is also always present, always able to be heard. Right here and right now, the Holy One of Being is saying the very same words that were said at Sinai. This poses two problems: If Torah is being spoken all the time, then why can't we hear it? And, if Torah is being spoken all the time, what is so special about the revelation at Sinai!? KiTov answers both questions with a daring insight into the nature of consciousness.

The reason Sinai is so special and the reason why we are unable to hear Torah all the time, he suggests, is because the noise, static, and muzak of this world drown out the sound of God's voice. Only at the time of the "giving of the Torah" did God "silence the roar." In the language of modern sound-recording technology, God, you might say, switched on the "Dolby" noise reduction system. At Sinai we could hear what had been there (and continues to be here) all along.

God is the One who enables us to hear what is being spoken at the most primary levels of reality. Each act of conscious focus is a miniature Sinai that now can be in every place.

THIS VERY PLACE

In rabbinic tradition, the Hebrew word for "place," *makom*, is also a name for God. This occasions some fascinating word plays. According to the Midrash,

> [When] the brothers of Joseph saw that their father was dead...they were afraid. They saw that at the time they were returning from burying their father, Joseph went to offer a blessing at that pit into which [they]...had thrown him. And he offered a blessing over it, as one is obligated to do at a place where a miracle has been done for him: "Blessed be the *makom* [the Place? God?] who made a miracle for me in this place." (*Tanhuma*, version A, *Vayechi* 17, end)

Likewise, in the story of Jacob's dream, we read that he "came upon the place/*makom*." One midrash, punning on the word *makom*, suggests that it means that Jacob came upon God! (*Pirke deRabbi Eliezer*, ch. 35) Another midrash cites a teaching of Rabbi Huna, who taught in the name of Rabbi Ammi, and makes the misreading into theology:

> Why do we change the name of the Holy One, and call God *makom* [the Place]? Because God is the place of the world and not the other way around. Rabbi Jose bar Halafta said: We do not know whether God is the place of the world or whether the world is God's place, but from the verse, "Behold, there is a place with Me" (Exodus 33:21), it follows that the Lord is the place of the world, but this world is not God's place. (*Bereshit Rabba* 68:9)

God, the Holy One of Being, is more than everywhere; God is the Ground of the World's Being, the very Place of Being itself. And to be awake and present "in this place" is to encounter God. In Rashi's words, as he comments on the verse in Exodus (33:21), "On the mountain where I speak with you always, there is a place prepared by Me for your sake where I will hide you so that you will not be injured. From there you will see what you will be permitted to see. This is its simple meaning."

Jacob must have remembered his father Isaac, and his grandfather Abraham, and the terrible mountain they called Moriah—"the place where God will be seen." According to one rabbinic legend, it was in this same ubiquitous place, unbeknown to Jacob, that he fell asleep and had his dream.

BEING PRESENT

You already are where you need to be. You need go nowhere else. Find a point an inch or so behind your sternum where your heart beats. That is where the *makom*, the place, is. Right here all along and we did not know it because we were fast asleep, here in this very *makom*.

In the panentheism of the Hasidic revival, as Rabbi Menachem Nahum of Chernobyl taught, "All being itself is derived from God and the presence of the Creator is in each created thing."[7] Or in the words of Rabbi Aryeh Leib of Ger, "A person is able to awaken the holiness of God in any place."[8]

Rabbi Menachem Mendel of Kotzk observed that the verse in Exodus seems to be redundant. God says to Moses, "Come up to Me on the mountain and be there." (Exodus 24:12) If Moses were to ascend the mountain, why would God also bother to specify that he "be there"? Where else would he be? The answer, suggests the Kotzker, is that people often expend great effort in climbing a mountain, but once they get there, they're not there; they're somewhere else![9]

Entrances to Holiness

ENTRANCES TO HOLINESS ARE EVERYWHERE.
The possibility of ascent is all the time.
Even at unlikely times and through unlikely places.
There is no place on earth without the Presence.
(*Bamidbar Rabba* 12:4)

Jacob, our father, was on the run. With only a rock for a pillow. In what he thought was some God forsaken wilderness. Until he had the dream of the ladder joining heaven and earth. "Surely the Holy One Himself, must have been in this very place and I didn't even know it!" And then he was afraid. He said, "How awesome is this place. This is none other than God's house and here I am at the very doorway to heaven!" (Genesis 28:16–17)

In another place we read of how the Holy One chose a common insignificant thorn bush. As if to teach us that nothing is beneath being a gateway to the Most High. He could have summoned mountains or oceans or the heavens themselves. But instead He "opened" a bush. "And [Moses] looked and behold the bush was on fire but the bush was not consumed." (Exodus 3:2)

How long must someone look at a burning bush to know whether or not it is being consumed! Certainly longer than most people look at anything. Longer, in other words, than you need to. More than to see it. Or to use it. Long enough to see if it will be for you an Entrance. Such a man was Moses, our teacher. And likewise, anyone who is able to gaze on a place long enough without being distracted.

Once there was a man who could enter higher worlds merely by drawing a circle in the earth and standing within it. "I can do nothing very well except draw circles and stand in them," he would say. "But the circles are as perfect as are humanly possible and I can station myself within them without distraction." And so the Holy One would come out of hiding. Such a man was Honi, the circle drawer. (*Taanit* 19a) In a wilderness. Through a bush. From a circle. Nothing is beneath the dignity of being selected as an entrance.

"Remove your shoes from your feet for the place upon which you are standing is holy ground." (Exodus 3:5) Not that ground then. But this ground now. Not Jacob or Moses or Honi. But you who are reading these lines.

You do not have to go anywhere to raise yourself. You do not have to become anyone other than yourself to find entrances. You are already there. You are already everything you need to be. Entrances are everywhere and all the time. "There is no man who does not have his hour and no thing that does not have its place." (*Avot* 4:3)

THE FIRST SNOW

One day I visited my daughter's first grade class. There was a teacher and her assistant and myself. And eighteen souls who have been present for but six winters. The air hung with a November chill. The children were work/playing in four or five groups, when the mist outside turned imperceptibly into snowflakes. "Look! It's snowing outside!" one shouted. "Winter is here!" And the groups crumbled as their members ran to the windows. No need for daily prayer here. Or for the proper blessing on seeing nature's wonders for the first time. Not for them. But for me! "Praised are You, O Holy wonderful Lord, Master of the universe, who makes things like this."

"Quick Daddy! Help me on with my coat. We're going outside!" And I stood at the window watching the snow fall on my little girl. There are places children go that grown-ups can only observe from afar.

The Shortest Proper Blessing

One *Shabbos* dinner our children were ill. We spent more time trying to pacify them than on making a holy meal. And, as so often
happens at such times, the end of the meal with its sharing and
singing and blessing simply disintegrated. I was left alone at the
table without even enough dedication to sing the final blessing. It
was then that I remembered that a friend had pointed out to me the
shortest ritually sufficient concluding prayer. He had even written
it down on a card that was somewhere in the study. I resolved to say
its five Aramaic words if only I could find it.

Once I located it, I realized that I had misspelled a word and
that I wasn't sure of the meaning of two others. First I had to search
out the phrase in the Talmud. Then I had to look up the words,
which by now had become very important. Now as it happens, God
gave me a good hand and I am something of a calligrapher. I decided to write the blessing in as beautiful a script as I could. I
convinced myself that the prohibition against writing on the Sabbath had not been intended to thwart so personal a mode of thanks.
Not only would I fix the words in my mind but I might, on this
confused evening, offer the work of my hands in gratitude.

It was one of those beautiful sunset evenings. The long shadows of the trees gently blowing in the evening breeze. And just as I
made the last dot I became aware that someone was in the room. I
looked up expecting to find Karen or one of the kids (who are very
good at sneaking up on you). But no one was there. Just a presence.
And the fading shadows. "Blessed be the compassionate One, Master of this bread." (*Berakhot* 40b)

The Museum Entrance

We once spent a week in Holland and during our visit to Amsterdam
stayed at a place called the Museum Hotel. From there we toured
the city and countryside and saw what I thought were all the sights.
From my garret window I even drew pictures of the great gabled

building across the street. And from one of those sketches I did one of the better paintings I have ever done. I gave that oil to one of my teachers and when I last saw it, it was hanging in his front hallway. But it was only a few years ago that I learned that our hotel drew its name from the Rijks Museum and that I had painted a picture of one of the great painting halls of the world. For even though I must have passed its door tens of times, I did not know I was passing the entrance to the Rijks Museum. I guess I was not then ready.

Graves on the Side of a Hill

Once we made our way down the hundreds of steps leading to the old cemetery of Safed. High in the Galilean hills, the town was for centuries the center of Judaism's greatest mystical revival. Buried on the side of the mountain lies Rabbi Isaac Luria, the Lion, the *Ari*, creator of Lurianic Kabbala. So many visitors have come to light a candle here and, an old folk custom of respect, deposit a pebble that the place is covered with stones and melted wax. And scrawled notes and crumpled prayers. And except for the unending breeze from the valleys below, there is stillness. Next to Luria is Alkabetz, author of *Lecha dodi*, the great Sabbath hymn. On the other side is Joseph Karo, author of the *Shulchan Aruch*, the great Code of Law. It was here that we found ourselves. Although we were not sure why we had come. And then after a few moments, we understood.

The memories of a place become a part of it. Places and things never forget what they have been witnesses to and vehicles of and entrances for. What has happened there happened nowhere else. Like ghosts who can neither forget what they have seen nor leave the place where they saw it, such are the memories tied to places of ascent. Temples. Trees. Melodies. Objects. Words. Whatever they have witnessed is chiseled into their substance.

Holy gates are everywhere. People come who would sell us tickets to the holy places. Who perhaps once and perhaps still, but probably never, were themselves graced to witness or themselves to ascend higher. Culture and organized religion conspire to trick us into believing that entrances to holiness are only at predictable times and prearranged places. (Sometimes they are right.) Otherwise people would not pay their dues. And most of us professional holy people would have to set out again in search of the Nameless One.

The cycle alternates between grand cathedrals and meditation amidst the trees of the forest. When people become convinced that the places and the things are themselves holy or that only some people have the spiritual power, then it is time once more to set out for and rediscover the fundamental truth: Entrances to holiness are everywhere and all the time.

This Is Your Life

WHEN I WAS GROWING UP, there was a TV show during which they'd bring an unsuspecting soul out of the studio audience and tell his or her life story. It was creatively called, "This Is Your Life." The master of ceremonies would recount part of a story and from off stage you would hear a little old lady say, "I remember the way you used to sit in the back row of my geometry class and throw paper airplanes at the little blonde girl across the aisle." Whereupon the guest of honor would say something like, "Oh my God, it's Mrs. Connley!" And Mrs. Connley would come out from behind the curtain and they would hug and usually cry. The master of ceremonies would tell a few more stories and introduce a few more mystery guests until the past joined the present and the guest's life was told. Then, the show was over. It took a half hour.

Deprived of a television program, the rest of us are left instead to review our lives through a hodgepodge of stories that describe what we think we have done and what we think has been done to us. Only rarely does it make sense.

There is a fascinating passage near the end of Deuteronomy: "And not until this day has God given you a heart to understand, eyes to see, or ears to hear. I led you through the wilderness forty years and the clothes on your back did not wear out..." In other words, for the four prior decades the children of Israel had wandered clueless around the wilderness and never had to shop for clothes. Sounds odd, if you ask me.

Simcha Bunam, one of the early Hasidic masters, explains that this passage means that the Israelites did not understand what God did during those forty years because everything that happened was unique to that particular time. There had never been anything like it before; there would never be anything like it again. The wandering Israelites of Sinai never figured out what was going on because it never dawned on them that they were players in a sacred story.

At the end of forty years, however, the Jews realized that religious history was about to be clothed in their deeds, made from whatever they had done. Not only from the holy moments, but from the mundane, the wayward, even the sinful moments as well. Imagine, ultimate truth clothed in the stories of your life. (This, indeed, *is* your life.)

Now if you protest that the deeds of your life are simply too irreligious to be included in such a holy book, take comfort in the behavior of everyone from Adam through Joshua: murderers, lechers, liars, cheats, thieves. As Hanan Brichto, professor of Bible at Hebrew Union College, used to quip, there's no one in the Hebrew Bible you'd want your kid to grow up to be like.

And the wilderness generation, that wacky, zany band of irreligious forty-year wanderers—who, with their own eyes, saw the Red Sea split and Moses ascend Mount Sinai, who ate manna for breakfast and quail for supper—these were the ones who built the golden calf, denied God at every opportunity, begged to go back to Egypt, and committed adultery with every tribe they met. These exemplary spiritual specimens were privileged to have the serial rights to their life story chosen for the script of the most holy document ever recorded.

So there's hope for you and me, yet. But alas, for most of us, only at the end of forty years do we begin to understand that even *our* life stories are sacred, that no television show could possibly comprehend them, and that God has been involved all along. Reverence is the only option.

ORIGINALLY PUBLISHED IN *MOMENT* MAGAZINE, APRIL 1993

"Into the Sea on Dry Ground"

ALL OF PASSOVER IS CONCEALED within one phrase: "And the children of Israel went into the midst of the sea on dry ground." (It comes up three times in Exodus 14, once in 15, and again in Nehemiah 9.) The whole thing is crammed into one literally impossible, delicious self-contradiction. You can either be "in the midst of the sea" or you can be "on dry ground." But you cannot be both "in the midst of the sea" *and* "on dry ground" at the same time. (Unless, of course, you are in another universe. More about that later.)

We say after a quick reading that the text obviously means that once the children of Israel arrived at sea, then it became dry ground or perhaps, as the famous midrash about Nahshon ben Aminadav teaches, once they stepped into the midst of the sea up to their nostrils, then it became dry ground. But that is not what Torah says. It says they did both and at the same time!

When I was a little boy growing up in Detroit, my mother always shopped at I think it was called the "Big Bear Market" because they gave S & H Green Stamps. These were the grocery store precursors of frequent traveler air miles. These stamps came in small perforated and gummed sheets and were awarded in proportion to each dollar spent. It was my job to lick the stamps and paste them into little newsprint booklets about the size of a TV Guide. We kept the booklets fat with stamps in a shoe box on the floor of the front hall closet, and when the box was full we would take its contents to the local S & H Green Stamp "Redemption" Center, where we would exchange this basically worthless stash of stickum for something of more enduring value like a carpet sweeper or an electric toaster. That is how I came to learn about redemption: the process of cashing in your chips or exchanging something for its true worth. Stamps for toasters or slaves for free men and free women, it's all the same. But you can't have one until you relinquish the other.

In Kabbalistic thought this is called "entering the *ayin*," or the "Holy Nothingness." In order for something to change from what it is into whatever it hopes to become there must be a moment when it has stopped being what it was yet before it has become what it hopes to become. For a split second it is literally nothing. No longer Green Stamps, no longer slaves. Not yet toasters, not yet free men and free women. And when we say that *Pesach* is the great festival of death and rebirth it is just this Holy Nothingness that effectuates the transformation. The metaphors for it are everywhere, from the symbolic "birth" of walking through a doorway smeared with the blood (of a lamb?) the morning after the first seder to, as Professor Lawrence Hoffman has demonstrated, the *matzah* as a replacement for the Pascal offering connoting salvation—to take this bread into you and be transformed. But none of them are as literally overwhelming as passing through the sea (of amniotic waters).

Indeed, it has always seemed to me that the miracle was not that the waters parted for the Israelites but that they all walked into the midst of sea, drowned, and were reborn free men and women on the other side. You want to be reborn, you want that a new and better you should emerge from the frozen hulk winter has made you, you want to be free again? Then you have let go of the old you. You must be willing to walk into the midst of the sea on dry ground and risk it all. But you say, "What if I don't come out the other side?" And I say there were probably a lot of Jews who were also afraid to step into the midst of the sea. They chose instead to bank on old, but sure slave lives. We never heard from them again. But the ones who entered the water, hungry for a rebirth were rewarded. Not with the Promised Land but with the strange honor of being able to wander in the wilderness for forty years. Theirs was the ultimate act of faith and may be been rewarded with the ultimate gift: rebirth in the wilderness.

At the core of this great feast of redemption is the preposterous assertion that the redemption of the children of Israel did not occur until they entered a mode of being in which they were simultaneously and impossibly both slave and free, wet and dry, dead and alive. Perhaps this is why, as the *Haggadah* reminds us, every Jew must regard him or herself as if he or she were personally a slave in Egypt. But how could that be, here we are sitting around a banquet table as free men and women! To live in the paradox.

My Father and "The Thing"

SOMETIMES MOVIES SHOW US MORE THAN THEY KNOW. When I was eight years old, for instance, my father took me to the Fox Theater in Detroit. My mother planned that it would be a special afternoon for just me and my dad. The afternoon was special all right but not in the way she had in mind.

We saw a black-and-white science fiction movie called "The Thing." (They came out with a remake of it a few years ago.) As clearly as I can recollect, it was about how this flying saucer crashed up in the Arctic wilderness and its only occupant, a monster from outer space, terrorized the scientists at an isolated research outpost. I still remember a few details. The eight-foot-tall "thing" was neither animal nor mineral, but rather had the same chemical composition as a carrot. (At the time this was *not* at all humorous.) In the last scene that I saw, the hulking, alien creature, impervious to gunfire, arms swinging at its sides, lumbered down a long corridor toward the terrified scientists. I don't know what happened after that. I was so frightened I told my father I had to use the men's room. In the lobby I found several other people also waiting it out, many of whom were chain smoking.

That evening, before it was time for me to go to sleep, my parents and I sat on the living room floor playing a board game. But I was distracted and kept glancing nervously down the darkened hallway leading to my bedroom. Under interrogation, I confessed that I was afraid to go to bed alone, and then the whole story about "The Thing" came out.

"What on earth ever possessed you to take him to a monster movie?" whispered my mother.

"I dunno," shrugged my father. "I figured he'd like it..."

For the next few weeks, my dad had to sit with me at night in my bedroom until I fell asleep. As I grew older, it became something of a joke between us, but to this day I still don't watch monster movies.

Recently, I wound up at two spiritual retreats, back to back. The first was a weekend at a Jewish New Age conference center, the second was for three days of silent meditation at a Buddhist retreat. They were both wonderful experiences. If I had any complaint at all, it would be that, as a carnivore, I found it difficult to go without meat for the better part of a week.

The Buddhist place was in rural Massachusetts. There was a lounge and meditation hall on the upper level, and on the lower there were fourteen monastic cells and lavatories for the retreatants. My room was the last one on the left side of a long corridor. Just beyond my room, at the end of the hallway, was a glass doorway through which you could see a field. We spent virtually all of our waking hours learning about silence and how to "mindfully" sit in stillness or walk in slow motion. Conscious of every breath, conscious of every step, trying to be fully present in each moment. I really got into it.

Even though it wasn't required, walking consciously, deliberately, and slowly had a kind of momentum that continued beyond the exercises. I found myself taking a long time to walk everywhere, to meals, to the sessions, even to the bathrooms at the other end of the hallway in the middle of the night. This self-imposed discipline created one minor problem: For the first two nights, I didn't realize until it was too late that no one had remembered to shut off the bright lights in the hall. So, on the third night, before going to sleep, I made a special point of turning off the overhead lights. This had one unforeseen and terrifying effect.

With only the nightlights on now, the glass doorway at the end of the hall became a kind of two-way mirror. Someone inside could see both outside *and* a reflection of himself mirrored on the glass, and someone (I imagined) on the outside could see both inside *and* a reflection of himself. So, on that third night, I could easily watch myself, in slow motion, walking back to my room. Conscious of every step. One step at a time. Arms swinging slowly at my sides.

It took me a few minutes to comprehend the image I beheld in the glass door, but once I did, I shuddered with reverence. The vision before me, my reflection in that screen, looked just like, you guessed it, "The Thing"! Only now it wasn't an alien space monster I was watching in a movie. I was watching *myself*. That creature, deliberately walking down the hallway, arms swinging slowly at his sides—and after five days of abstaining from meat, made entirely of vegetables—was me! (For all I know there was an eight-year-old little boy and his father outside in the wintry field watching what *they* thought was only a monster movie, when in fact they were actually peering into the little boy's future.)

And then I understood: My father, his memory is a blessing, had taken me, forty-five years ago, to the Fox Theater to see *myself* as a fifty-three-year-old rabbi lumbering down the hallway of a Buddhist retreat center on his way back to bed—preoccupied with remaining conscious of each present moment. So I thanked my father and went to sleep without being afraid.

Words of Fire

JUDAISM BEGINS WITH GOD SAYING TO MOSES at Mount Sinai, "Here, take this book home and read it. Let me know what you think." Reading, reflecting, studying for Jews may be the primary religious act. Each book is a symbol of what transpired in the Sinai wilderness. That would explain why the bookshelves in synagogue prayer halls are filled with more than prayerbooks and why it is not uncommon, during a prayer service, to find a few people at the back of the room studying. Study is a meditative and transformative act.

Think of sacred text as a "word" spoken to a therapist. And the question to the therapist is, what does it mean? (Once you know the answer, the therapy is probably complete.) But how to find the meaning? Who said it? In what context? Who was the intended audience? What associations do the words have? Indeed, when understood through contemporary deconstructionism, "meaning" does not reside in words, it is "constructed" by the reader. Many observers, notably Dr. Susan Handelman, author of *Slayers of Moses*, have suggested that rabbinic tradition is the precursor of modern literary theory with its refusal to assign absolute meaning to any statement.

Everything remains fluid; certainty is simply out of the question. The midrashic approach to sacred text sees the biblical word as the repository of an infinity of meanings. Every word, indeed, every letter, is an entryway to meaning. Through allusion, association, imagination, secret, mystical tradition, we are ultimately led to literally every other biblical word, or, to borrow an image from the internet, hypertext.

According to one tradition there were 600,000 Jews at Mount Sinai and there were therefore 600,000 meanings to the Torah! To make things even more complicated, since we all change from one day to the next, each time the Torah is (re-)read in the synagogue, it is a new Torah. People, in other words, don't read the thing year in and year out to rehearse the story but to discover what they missed last year. The sacred text becomes, as it were, a kind of refractive lens through which we discover who we are. But there is more.

Not only is the text infinitely analyzable and perpetually in motion, it is an instrument of our own self-discovery and enlightenment. According to one legend, a seeker is granted permission to glimpse heaven. There he sees an academy filled with rows of paired students studying sacred text. "Are they in Heaven?" the seeker asks. "No," comes the reply. "Heaven is in them." In this way, through the reverent study of holy words anything becomes possible. All doorways are open.

The Letter Lammed

LAMMED, OH SO BEAUTIFUL *LAMMED*. Tall and elegant like a palm branch, *lulav* waved high.

Lammed is a student. At night, *lilah*, by the moon, *l'vanah*, forever, *l'olam*, while everyone else is asleep, *lammed* studies the holy books.

Yet while its body may be curled in the midst of the study place, its heart, *laev*, soars like a flame, *lahav*, above all the other letters. From the wisdom to see ahead comes the strength to say, no. "Thou shalt not," *lo*. An idol says, yes. Always, yes. But one who studies the words of the Living God also hears, "Thou shalt not." So the *lammed* was chosen to say, no.

Come my beloved, *lecha dodi*, *lammed*. Teach me. Study with me. Tell me of the thirty-six righteous ones, *lammed vav tsaddikim*, who carry in their hearts the pain of all the world.

If you understand how bread, *lechem*, and flame, *lahav*, and to learn, *lomed*, and heart, *laev*, all *share* in *lammed*, then perhaps you are also a *lammed*.

The Law Is a Way

THE WAY IS NOT A BOOK OR A SCROLL. The Way is a perfect description of all Being. And, since it is perfect, The Way is also the same as All Being. The description, in other words, is identical with The Way itself. Because The Way comes from The Source of All Being, trying to understand The Way constitutes the highest activity of mind, just as living in accordance with it is the highest expression of right behavior. In the words of the Proverb: "She is a tree of life to those who hold fast to her."

The Way is the master code for all creation, the infra-structure of being, the blueprint for the world, the source of each person's self. So, in an important sense, to learn about The Way is also to learn about yourself. But you must listen with great care and remove all distracting noise.

Any other noise will drown it out. This was the very same whisper Elijah the prophet heard when he stood on the place where Moses stood and heard the thin, barely audible sound of almost breathing.

This quiet sound and the sustained, silent attention that renders it audible and intelligible place demands on human behavior. To ignore these demands is more than abdicating an existential responsibility. It constitutes sin.

An Orchard of Holy Words

HOW COULD EVERYTHING YOU NEED TO KNOW be contained in the Torah, in only five books? Long ago our teachers realized that the Torah is like a beautiful orchard. From a distance you see only a field of trees. When you come closer, you see that each has leaves, blossoms, and fruit. When you come even closer, you realize that a skin covers each fruit. And, if you are persistent and peel back the skin, your reward is a delicious treat. Now you realize that what at first seemed to be only a field of trees actually conceals layers within layers of wonderful things.

The Hebrew word for orchard is *pardes*, spelled: *pey, resh, dalet, samech*. Each one of these letters stands for a layer of the Torah.

The letter *pey* is the first letter of *peshat*, which means the simple story, the one you find if you just read the Torah quickly without much thought. When Adam disobeyed God and ate from the tree of knowledge, he was ashamed, so he hid himself. (Genesis 3:8–10) That is the simple story.

The letter *resh* is the first letter of *remez*, which means hint. If you think about a story or a word in the Torah, it usually will lead to your thinking about something else. As you wonder what the word means, you might notice that it reminds you of something you have thought about or done in the past. Perhaps, like Adam, you once did something you were ashamed of and tried to hide. Adam's story hints at something in your life.

The letter *dalet* is the first letter of *derash*, which means "interpreting." Some of the lessons in the story may remind you of other stories in the Torah, which, in turn, can teach you about your life. If God knows where Adam is hiding, then why ask him, "Where are you?" Perhaps God wants Adam to realize that, when he tries to hide from God, he is hiding only from himself.

The letter *samech* is the first letter of *sod,* which means secret. This layer is "secret," not because it cannot be told, but because, even when seen, its meaning remains mysterious. Only an advanced student of Torah can understand the "secret" meaning when God says, "Yesterday, Adam, you were so big that you extended from one end of the universe to the other, but now, after you have sinned, you can hide among the trees of the garden." (*Bereshit Rabba* 19:9)

Taken all together, *pey, resh, dalet,* and *samech* (the simple, the hint, the interpreting, and the secret) spell *Pardes,* orchard. The Torah, the source book of Judaism, is like an orchard; it conceals many wonderful and delicious surprises. But, more than that, it tells us everything we, as Jews, need to know and do. By telling us how to live, Torah gives us life. Just as it says in the Book of Proverbs (3:18), "It is a tree of life to those who hold on to it."

Like Ones in a Dream

NO ONE REALLY KNOWS WHAT DREAMS ARE—hallucinatory wish fulfillment, the voice of the collective unconscious, a continuous process parallel to consciousness, random sorting of overloaded memory circuits, the medium of prophecy, or the mind's struggle to circumvent the formal law of contradiction. But everyone dreams anyway. And we—from Joseph to Daniel to Freud—have had dreams, read them, interpreted them, hidden from them, and even, on occasion, faithfully chanted them from a handwritten parchment scroll. They are an intimate part of our lives.

The Bible is another story. For all its ubiquity and all our devout attention, it remains worlds away. So far away that its sanctity no longer awes; its humanity no longer humbles; the mode of consciousness it might once have evoked no longer possible. What once was the place where humanity and the One of Being might peer into each other's minds, perhaps sharing a moment or two, seems lost. We need a metaphor, an intermediate place between creature and Creator. Ironically, even though the Bible itself is precisely that metaphor, we continue to search elsewhere. In our own day, several metaphors enjoy a wide currency. Each one has its own insight and clarifies another dimension of a mode of consciousness that, finally, can have no direct expression. We say that Scripture is like great religious literature. But that removes the possibility of its holiness, and consequently undermines the worth of any particular religion's tradition of understanding the biblical text. Some have suggested that the Bible is like a marriage contract. This recovers some of the holiness and intimacy, but ultimately fails, inasmuch as no one religiously studies the terms of a marriage. Or we say that the Bible is like history or archaeology or culture; in this way we may learn history or archaeology or culture, but not Bible. Or we say that the Bible is like an anthology of ethical teachings; unfortunately, many of the Bible's obvious ethical teachings are patently unacceptable. Sometimes we give in to that precious nagging human need for a higher authority and side with orthodox fundamentalist tradition in claiming that the whole thing is simply, literally true and that the Holy One of Being wrote it word for word. But by insisting on such a crystalline reading of what are inescapably human words, we only make a travesty of the holy lights they must obviously conceal. There is even a metaphor in which we liken ourselves to the pious ones of old. This works as long as we can go on pretending. And so it is that we spend most of our time not learning Bible, but apologizing for it, becoming servants of our own metaphors.

We seek a metaphor for holy words that will return them to us once again as an *aytz chayim*, a tree of life (Proverbs 3:18). One that yields heightened self-awareness *and* God's Word. One that per- mits sustained intellectual inquiry *and* Scripture's holiness. One that pre- serves clarity, but not at the expense of mystery. One whose playfulness does not dilute piety. One whose public objectivity tol- erates personal intimacy. In the spiritual code words of our generation: a holy text.

THE GREAT DREAM

If a group of people can have a psyche and think of itself as an organic being, then surely a people should also be able to dream. A series of motifs and archetypes should keep reappearing and seem to each individual dreamer, as Jung suggested, to emanate from a transcendent source. God would be present in those dreams, even as God speaks to and is within the people themselves. Johannes Pedersen, the Danish Bible scholar, in describing the biblical mind— our group mind of an earlier time—observes that, while "the dream is a communication from God to man...it does not clash with the psychological process. The dream is a communication from God because it is a direct outcome of reality itself."[1]

And this is how it goes. In each generation there are encounters with the Holy Ancient One of Old. Visioned and recorded almost unconsciously. And some encounters, by reason of their terror or subtlety, simply go unrecorded. Fragments remembered the next morning at breakfast. Slid through the cracks. Finding their way to the dream-memory of the people. And then it happens that one of the people writes, sings, legislates, scolds, or simply remembers. Perhaps with some awareness of destiny, or maybe just to earn a living. No matter. Each is organically part of us, an instrument of the Word. And their collective bringing-to-our-attention is the great dream.

Scripture, then, might be understood as what has been saved for us of our collective memory. A remnant of the work of ten thousand censors. And several dozen poets, prophets, and teachers. The last of these may have been our parents (who read the Bible to us, although perhaps with a different intention). A kind of journal of forgotten, reworked, and remembered holy moments, too awesome to be simply described in everyday conscious language. It is all that remains of the most penetrating incursion of waking into the earth-mother-Jewish-people darkness of what is not the spirit, but only sleep. But the memory is still there, set in our bodies by our parents or our choice.

We may ignore the dream or we may appropriate it for ourselves, and so make it our own. It is our choice alone.

Scripture is the result of the attempt to bring to the life light of consciousness the latent, unresolvable dialectic of unconsciousness. The left cerebral hemisphere's futile foray into the right side. Rational language's hopeless try at putting in a simple proposition what can only be said in a disjunctive one. Or, as it is told that Abraham Joshua Heschel taught about all holy stories, "An occasion when the heart surprises the mind."

Now this common dream is more than a mythic belief system: it is part of our very being. And this, then, is the job of the searchers and the dreamers: to reach deeper and deeper into the dream. Peeling away one layer after another. Until we realize that the voice speaking our dreams comes from within us and from without at the same time. Until we see at last that the story is true. Not necessarily because it happened in a particular place at a particular time, but because it is within us. It always was. It issues from us. It is ours. It is something we know from our innermost being. Even as it echoes the One who spoke the first letter that had no sound. It is our dream. It is a holy text.

Both Bible and dream are first encountered as mystery, and in the final interpretation remain mystery. For both are inexhaustible and infinitely analyzable. "It is a fragment of a dream we get under all circumstances."[2]

Both Bible and dream are multi-layered. Intelligible as the manifest *peshat,* simple shell of the fruit. And yet, upon closer observation, concealing a myriad of deeper layers. Each one somehow protecting the latent *sod,* secret seed within.

Both Bible and dream create their own internal logic and systems of space and time. There is no before or after in the Torah. (*Pesachim* 7b)

In both Bible and dream, nothing is accidental. The most trivial detail or the most nonsensical pun is there for a reason.

In both Bible and dream the story and the characters and even the very words and letters themselves are contorted, convoluted, condensed, inverted, rearranged, and often out of place. But we do not dismiss such a dream.

Both Bible and dream are creations from the innermost depths of our collective and individual beings. Creations of our ancient memories of holy history that seem to hint at the ultimate nature of reality.

Both Bible and dreams seem to issue from outside ourselves. Whether from the collective memory, or, as Zalman Schachter Shalomi has suggested, a letter we have written to ourselves from some previous incarnation, or the word of God.

Both Bible and dream, in moments of understanding, seem to come from inside us. Some thin, barely audible sound of almost breathing (1 Kings 19:12), a way each of us has of talking with ourselves privately. Whether Freud's hallucinatory wish fulfillment or the voice of religious inspiration.

And both Bible and dream share an ability to synthesize the external, communal, and public dimension of life with its internal, private, and personal side. Indeed, from Jung to Freud, or from mystic to rationalist, both Bible and dream are understood by parallel spectra of interpretations.

SCRIPTURE AND OTHER DREAMS

Suppose Scripture were like a dream, and we were its vessels. Like ones in a dream. If Scripture be like a dream, then methods of understanding the dream are, at least in principle, valid for learning Scripture. Let us consider some of the modes of dream interpretation. Ten classic entrances to the dream. Ten ways of considering our own conscious spiritual creation. For, by understanding our dream, we understand more than Scripture. We understand ourselves.

1. Begin with the most difficult and subtle question of all. One that will now through successive answers as our own self-awareness deepens: What is the underlying emotional dynamic of the story? When viewed from a distance, what is the feel of the dream's prevailing emotion? What holds it together? Keeps our interest?

2. Recall our own recent experiences. Since dreams are often initiated by something that happened recently, we must ask about

yesterday's residue. What were the extraordinary events that startled our consciousness and sparked the dream?

3. Isolate and identify the primary elements of the dream text before us. What are the dream's components? One of the most common errors made in trying to understand a dream is the almost automatic refusal to recognize more than one character or element or verbal idea in the narrative, when of course, all the parts are indispensable.

4. Pay especially close attention to the seemingly trivial details and the little discrepancies. If teachers and interpreters who preceded us were unafraid to seek significance in puns, letter arrangement, or even the tiny crownlets of the ancient Hebrew script, then neither should we. Seemingly trivial words conceal the entrance to a deeper meaning.

5. We must not allow embarrassment to distract attention from elements that make us uncomfortable. Disgust and dread are the sorts of feelings we frequently marshal to conceal deeper layers of our psyche.

6. If this Scripture dream is actually ours, then our associations are relevant. Often, they will obviously be of only personal validity, but at other times they will open new dimensions of understanding as compelling as those of commentators of old. What first occurs to us on remembering the dream/reading the text may be the most important thing. The key itself.

7. Assume full responsibility for the dream. For "through the dream the man makes the matter his own; it is in his will, and he is responsible for it."[3] We usually hide from our dreams by thinking of ourselves as passive movie screens upon which they are shown. We

refuse to believe that they are our own meticulous creations, which we as individual dreamers or heirs of a particular spiritual tradition have authored. But to place anything in the scripture/dream outside ourselves is only to align ourselves with the wicked son of the *Haggadah's* Passover story, who denies any part in the tale. If the dream is confused, then it is we who have confused it. "The teaching of God is complete." (Psalm 19:8) That is, it is in the form it is supposed to be. If the dream has an evil side, then it is also a side of us. We are responsible for the evil impulses of our dreams.

8. The dream can condense opposites into one truth. "Dreams show a special tendency to reduce two opposites to a unity… Anything in a dream may mean its opposite… We must therefore entertain the hypothesis that there is an important connection between being 'dialectical' and dreaming, just as there is between dreaming and poetry or mysticism."[4]

9. The many selves, who together comprise one self, often separate. They stand before us in stark relief. We must therefore be all the parts of our dream. If the Scripture dream is ours, then we have done more than "have it." We have made it. Everything in it comes from us. Each character. Each scene. Each object. We chose them. Wrote the lines, or at least recorded them and not others. Abraham and Ur. Sacrifices and Sinai and blood and God and Moses and, yes, even Pharaoh. For he, too, is in us. As any good teacher of dreams will tell you, you are all the people in your dream. Fritz Perls taught, "[All] the different parts, any part in the dream—is yourself, is a projection of yourself."[5] And to ask why we made our story this way and not that way is to reenter our sacred text once again as living participants. We could have made it another way, but chose to cast it in this one. We must be all the parts of our dream, even the ones we don't like.

10. Through the dream/Scripture, we slip back to our origins. Through that infinity of meanings, we return to the undifferentiatedness of all existence. Another earlier (perhaps earliest) order of being, which not only punctuates our sleep but (we intuit) continuously flows beneath waking. This is the great dream of which each individual dream is a personal manifestation. Dream is ontogenetic. Myth is phylogenetic. "Dreams and especially myths are a primary medium for intuitive insights into the ultimate nature of human existence... [they] are not restricted to... sleep. They pertain rather to the symbolic dimension of human experience as a whole."[6]

To Live in the Dream

And then we awake to discover that the dreams we have dreamed are none other than the lives we live. In the words of the prophet Nathan (as he scolds David, the king, who has just been told an allegory of his life): "Thou art the man!" (2 Samuel 12:7) The story is not about someone else. It is not even about you. It is you. To live in the dream means that what Abraham once did is also for us to do.

To live through the dream means that what Abraham left undone might still be realized through our actions. And that what we witnessed last night is a truth we are trying to tell ourselves about ourselves, but are yet afraid to utter in the morning.

The dream is not static. Not something "out there." It has no fixed script, nor even a permanent past. It is constantly in motion. Perpetually flowing from us, just as our consciousness is never still. To utter the dream is to interpret it. And to interpret it is to change it. When we put into words something that did not happen in words, we give it a new and seemingly fixed image. Yet from day to day even the words themselves acquire new shades and subtleties. And to think about their meanings, so as to get a clearer understanding of them, is to step onto the dance floor before the music has stopped.

The dream is never still. It is infinitely analyzable, until finally, into that infinity of meanings, all the universe is drawn. Through the dream we enter into a relation with a hitherto unmet facet of being.

Perhaps there is another sense in which the dream creates us. The totality of all the dreams that have been dreamed or are yet to be work through us, with or without our individual or collective consent. With or without our knowledge. This consciousness, toward which we journey, flowing softly beneath everything, animating and filling our substance, speaks through us. And it joins us with all creation.

The one who pays attention to the dreams, draws on them, and lives them out is blessed. We each take our turn at living out the dream. Like some ageless wave, Scripture flows through us.

Not long ago, we dreamt the Bible. From deep within our several and collective unconsciousnesses, we brought it forth. Twisted, convoluted, and mysterious. But nevertheless true beyond our wildest dreams. Unable to withstand the going up from our depths, enough to remain in simple *peshat* form, it cloaked itself in mystery, transformed intolerable desires into dense imagery and words. Now all we have left is the piously handed down scroll, filled with square black letters, the spaces between them, and, of course, our own fragmented memories of a dream.

"Amemar, Mar Zutra and Rab Ashi would say this. Holy One of Being, I am yours and my dreams are yours. I have dreamed a dream and I do not know what it means…" (*Berakhot* 55b)

Fog

TWO SUMMERS AGO ED FELD AND I WENT SAILING out on Buzzard's Bay, or maybe I should say we tried to go sailing. On an otherwise clear and sunny afternoon, no sooner did we round green can #7 than such a dense fog set in you couldn't see Bird Island Light.

Now I love sailing and a good adventure as much as the next man, but only a fool would willingly pilot a small boat in fog. Even with instruments like global positioning system and radar, it's a dicey business. Fog disables more than your sense of sight; sounds too seem to come from the wrong directions. There simply are no longer any fixed points; certainty is out of the question. You have this weird sense that you are nowhere.

Fog is actually a fascinating atmospheric phenomenon. According to the *American Practical Navigator*, "Fog is a cloud whose base is low enough to restrict visibility. [It]…is composed of droplets of water…formed by condensation or crystallization of water vapor in the air." In other words, when you're in fog, your head is literally "in the clouds."

So that afternoon on Buzzard's Bay, there was nothing Ed and I could do but navigate out of the channel and out of harm's way, drop an anchor, and content ourselves with talking deep thoughts. I'd never seen it so bad. Unable to come up with an explanation, I observed with a wink, "Eddie, what can I say? You bring on the fog!"

This all reminds me of the weekly scriptural reading for this week in the synagogue. It comes from the concluding chapters of Exodus. It chronicles the consecration of the wilderness tabernacle and closes with a scene worthy of any great Hollywood production:

"The cloud of the Lord rested on the tabernacle...in the sight of all Israel, everywhere they wandered." (Exodus 40:38)

The great Italian Bible scholar of the last generation, Umberto Cassuto, observed that "the Tabernacle is a kind of miniature Sinai, which can be transported from place to place...[the intention seems to be] to link it with the first theophany...and to emphasize that this Divine revelation was not unique, but a recurring phenomenon."

So: the cloud makes the tabernacle a Mount Sinai, and since the tabernacle is mobile, the possibility of revelation is now ubiquitous. In meteorological terms, whenever the temperature goes below the dewpoint, condensation will occur. What an odd symbol for the divine presence: a cloud resting on the earth.

The Gaon (or "great sage") of Vilna, who was very wise but probably didn't know much about sailing a yacht in fog, juxtaposes two verses: Our verse, Exodus 40:38: "And the cloud of God was upon the tabernacle... everyone could see it" and Exodus 19:9 from the scene at Mount Sinai: "Behold, I come to you in a thick cloud so that all the people will hear My words with you..." I am struck by how he not only joins the wilderness tabernacle with Mount Sinai but also how he puts together the two senses, sight and hearing, which fog scrambles. It has something to do with the divine presence and a different kind of perception.

That is how teaching takes place in the Jewish community: The Torah or Scripture is expounded, interpreted, plumbed, allegorized, manipulated, massaged, psychoanalyzed, inverted, sliced, and diced. There is no one correct interpretation. Judaism may begin with a book, but it ends in the clouds. It is not a literal or fundamentalist tradition. Respect for teachers and text is expressed through arguing with them. The rabbis long ago understood this when they said that the stories in the Torah couldn't be about what they seem to be about, otherwise we could write better stories.

That is an important difference between literalism and metaphor. Literalism is clear, unequivocal, complete. Metaphor is suggestive, illusive, unsure of itself, unfinished, if you will, a little foggy. "And the Lord will appear in a cloud." In a cloud everything is up for grabs. According to the rabbis, each word of the sacred text has seventy faces and 600,000 meanings. Scripture, like Freud taught of any dream, is infinitely analyzable. And all the parts are essential—every word, every letter. There is, in principle, no distinction between the ten commandments and chapter 36 of Genesis, which delineates the progeny of Esau.

Gershom Scholem, the master historian of Jewish mysticism, once observed that in a revealed tradition, creativity must masquerade as commentary. That is to say that if God, at Mount Sinai, told people every thing worth knowing then all that remains is to explain, expound, and interpret it. You might say that Judaism commences with God saying to the Jewish people, "Here, take this book home, read it, and let Me know what you think."

The Zohar, the primary text of Kabbala, also cites Exodus 40:35: "'Moses was not able to enter into the tent of the congregation, because the cloud rested upon it,' and asks: What was that cloud?" It answers its own question: "It was a thread from the side of the primordial light, which, issuing forth joyously, entered the Divine presence and descended into the Tabernacle below. After the first day of creation it was never again made fully manifest, but it… daily renews the work of creation." So that was the cloud! A remnant of the primordial light of ultimate awareness created on the first day of creation, sealed away for the righteous of every generation.

Well, yes but no. According to the *Yoma* 4b: The school of Rabbi Ishmael notices that the word *b'tokh* ["into the midst of"] appears both in Exodus 24:18, where we read "And Moses entered into the midst of the cloud" and also in Exodus 14:22, "And the children of Israel went into the midst of the sea." It couldn't be accidental. Just as in one place the word *b'tokh* implies a path through the sea, so here too there must have been a path, for Moses through the cloud. So the cloud is more than a theophany and more than primordial light. It is also a path. And so you begin to understand about the 600,000 meanings. And in the Zohar we learn that "the cloud of the *Shekhinah* looked like smoke because the fire that Abraham and his son Isaac kindled clung to it and never left it, and by reason of that fire it ascended both as cloud and smoke..." Now it has become a cloud of smoke, mysteriously evoking the love and struggle between the generations.

The cloud, in other words, is a metaphor for the presence of God, but the metaphor also evokes the theophany of Mount Sinai, the primordial light of creation, the redemption at the Red Sea, and the love and struggle between the generations: "Behold, I come to you in a thick cloud..."

And that's what rabbis do, or at least try to do. They remind their students that the disorientation of being in the cloud may not be such a bad thing after all. We do have a tradition that the first Torah that God showed Moses was written in black fire on white fire. Not a text carved in stone. That's too hard, inflexible, strictly for Cecil B. De Mille. The Torah is not even a fixed text but a fiery, living organism. The Torah is the Name of God. And the Name of God is the Name of the Unity of All Being.

A rabbi is not an administrator, a CEO, a pastor, an educator, a professor, a charismatic, a shaman, or a politician. A rabbi is only one thing: a teacher. And the rabbi teaches only one thing: Torah: what God wants people to know, which is who and why they are. A rabbi, you might say, introduces people to the cloud of the divine presence and helps them not to be frightened of the disorientation that necessarily comes from realizing an infinity of meanings.

In religion and education, we speak approvingly of experiences that are clear or bright and of people who have them as knowing where they are and where they are going. And I suppose that most of the time that is wise and correct. But I must confess that as I think about it, there were times when I was confused, disoriented, and just plain lost, and that these turn out to have been even more important than all the others. The real growing, the real learning, begins when you are not sure where you are or where you are going: when you are in a fog. It's not knowing that's the goal.

I have a friend who has sailed across the Atlantic. He told me that a good navigator is never certain of his position. Even if he is standing under a street sign that says, "Fifth and Elm." "How could that be?" I asked. "Some kids as a prank might just have changed the sign."

We need to understand that the closest we come to getting a vision of God and therefore ultimate awareness is not necessarily radiance or sunshine or clarity but a lousy cloud: fog! That's how you can spot the presence of God: a cloud. Just water vapor condensing out of thin air. And eventually we understand from meteorologists and exegetes alike that clouds can and do appear virtually everywhere. And that is what we mean when we say, "the fog is in."

ORIGINALLY PUBLISHED IN *JUDAICA BOOK NEWS*, 1990

Reflections on the Holy Language

THE FIRST CLASS I EVER TAUGHT AS A RABBI was in Highland Park, Illinois. It was a beginning Hebrew class, one of those little groups that used to meet on a weekday morning twenty years ago when there were still a few women around who hadn't gone back to work or to school. For the first session, as a way of getting acquainted with one another, I went around the room and had people give their names and "share with the group" why they were learning Hebrew. The answers were beautiful but not surprising. One student wanted to be able to keep up with her child in religious school. Another wanted to be able to follow the prayers. A few people, God bless them, had their sights set on reading from the Torah. But one woman changed the meaning of the class for everyone.

After some careful thought and with a wry smile, she quietly said, "I don't think God is done talking and I think I believe that when God speaks again, it won't be in English." She didn't mean it in a chauvinistic way, she was just giving voice to what Jews have meant for centuries when they reserved Hebrew as the instrument for recording sacred text and uttering the words of prayer. She reminded us that Hebrew is the *l'shon kodesh*, the holy language. Or to put it another way, more than any other language, for us Jews, Hebrew "has to do with God."

Of course Hebrew is the language of religious business. But, even more important, Hebrew is the instrument through which the Torah is visible. And the Torah is the lens through which God is visible, just as the prayerbook is the lens through which the soul of the Jew is illumined.

On the Visual Array of Sacred Text

WE JEWS DIDN'T INVENT "TWO-POLLED" SCROLLS. They are simply an inevitable result of putting too much parchment on a single *megilla*. The second pole (to borrow an image from my generation's technology) is a "take-up reel." To my disappointment, I now un-derstand that we didn't even invent that visual arcade of commentary and argument epitomized by a page of Talmud. It was a creation of gentile typesetters. What we Jews seem to have given the world (to the dismay of fundamentalists everywhere) was the mischievous no-tion of a revealed tradition perpetually in flux, beautifully symbolized by a Torah scroll or a page of Talmud. But an even better metaphor for this comes from the way information is now routinely processed on the World Wide Web—you know, when the cursor changes from an arrow to a pointing finger whispering, "Click me, please." Doing so takes us somewhere else, perhaps in the same document or per-haps half-way around the world. These "blue words," which "turn an arrow into a human hand," are called "hypertext," words invis-ibly linked to some other non-contiguous text. Indeed, the whole idea of midrash (and maybe all Jewish education) seems predicated on this idea that ultimately, each word in scripture is connected to every other word. A mystical syntax in which every word is joined to every other word. A luminous organism of coherence, meaning, and unity: the body of God.

Reciting Psalms

AT A SUMMER INSTITUTE WHERE I WAS TEACHING a class on the meaning of sacred text, we studied a Hasidic story that taught that the text not only described, but actually contained the event itself. If read properly, the event could be summoned and relived. This reminded one student, Milt Zaiment, of something he had done as a boy more than sixty years before when his uncle had pneumonia.

"In those days, people didn't go to hospitals like they do now. My uncle lay in his bedroom and the doctor, a good man, came out and told my parents that the end was near. 'I'm sorry,' he consoled, 'but I don't expect him to live through the night.' We helped the doctor on with his coat and saw him to the door.

'Come,' said my father, taking me by the hand. 'We have a job to do.' He sat me down next to my uncle's bed, sat next to me, opened the Bible, and recited a psalm. Then he gave the book to me. 'Now you read.' When I finished, he took the book from me and read the next psalm. And so it went, all through the night, the two of us reciting psalms, one after another.

When morning came, my uncle was still alive. The doctor returned. He was amazed. He said he had never seen anything like it, that it was a miracle. My father smiled respectfully. He washed his face, had a cup of coffee, and went to work. He never said a word about that night. My uncle lived another forty years."

Arguing with Heaven

THE STORY IS TOLD OF RABBI LEVI YITZHAK OF BERDITCHEV that once on Kol Nidre, the holiest night of the year when all sins are confessed, the tailor, one of the most devout members of the community, was absent. Concerned, the rabbi left the synagogue and went to the tailor's home. To his surprise he found the tailor looking at a piece of paper before him on the table.

"What's the matter?" asked Levi Yitzhak.

"Oh, everything's fine," replied the tailor. "As I was getting ready to attend the service I made a list with two columns. At the top of one I wrote my name and at the top of the other I wrote, 'God of all the Universe.' Then, one by one, I began to list my sins. 'Cheated Goldman out of a pair of trousers.' And in God's column I noted God's omission: 'Little girl died of diphtheria.' Then the next sin, 'Lost my temper with my children,' and in God's column, 'I heard there was famine in another country.'" And so it went. The tailor showed the rabbi the completed list. "And for every sin I had committed during the past year, God had done one too. So I said to God, 'Look, we each have the same number of sins. If you let me off, I'll let You off.'"

But the story doesn't end there. When the rabbi looked at the paper his face grew red and he scolded his friend: "You fool! You had Him and you let Him go!"

Here is a kind of relationship with God unique to Jewish tradition. Jews don't just get angry with God. They call God to account. In Abraham's words, as he argues the fate of Sodom and Gomorrah, "Will You sweep away the innocent along with the guilty?... Shall not the Judge of all the earth deal justly?" (Genesis 18:23-35)

The man, in effect, is saying, "Just who the hell do You think You are?"

But there's another curve ball. If you believe, as I do, that "it's all God," then how do we argue with what we're made of? That destabilizes us, makes us very uncomfortable. It means we have to talk to ourselves. We no longer have the luxury of putting all the nasty decisions and deeds on some distant omniscient, omnipotent God, and freeing ourselves to bask in moral security. God says, in effect, "And whom do you think you're talking to? Hold up a mirror. When you're done with *that* conversation, come back to Me…"

The Letter Kaf

Kaf is the palm of hand filled with sincerity, *kavanah*.

Kaf is cup, *kos*, filled with blessing both for those who hold it and for those who drink from it.

It contains all the honor a child can bestow on his mother and father. *Kibbud ahv va-aim.* Honor of mother and father. That is all there is. *Kol.* All.

To take your parents seriously is the hardest commandment. To offer them the cup without spilling it. To receive from them the cup without gulping. Such is *kaf.* The cup of blessing. A goblet of honor. A crown, *keter*, for your head.

But only he shall drink who has himself spilled and gulped and wept.

Only he who has learned that not all intentions are as they seem.

Only he who is beaten, *kateet*, like oil that has been beaten from olives, until he is *kasher*, pure and fit, shall drink.

Then *kaf* transforms itself into the crown.

But of course once you have reached the rung of "the crown, *keter*," you would sooner give the crown to your mother and father. Never forget that your parents were the instruments God used to bring you into the world, and so must they be the instruments through whom you shall return to God.

Yeast in the Dough

NOTHING IS INTRINSICALLY EVIL. If something were, then God who is the Source of All Being could not be present everywhere in creation. If something were intrinsically evil, it would have to derive its reality from a force independent from God.

Even our ineluctable urge to do evil is not evil, but only misdirected. Indeed without it, as the legend goes, no hen would lay an egg, no house would be built, no one would go to work. There would be no babies. Psychological energy is mischievous. Left to itself, without direction, it would destroy the world. With direction and struggle, the same energy is a powerful force for healing and life. In the words of the sages, "The greater the person, the greater his or her propensity for doing evil."

We call this urge "the yeast in the dough," for like yeast it is ubiquitous, essential, even indispensable. This libidinous fermenting agent has as its principal weapon the art of disguise. No one in human history has ever set out to do something evil. Instead they believed what they were doing was right and proper. Our desire to label things as "good" or "bad," while of great value, is easily distorted. Most of the terrible things human beings do to one another, they do by telling themselves they are actually fighting against some external evil. But in truth more often than not they have only taken the evil into themselves and have become its agents.

The Hands of God

THE FOLLOWING STORY is told by my teacher, Rabbi Zalman Schachter Shalomi:

A long time ago in the northern part of Israel, in the town of Safed, the richest man in town was sleeping, as usual, through *Shabbat* morning services. Every now and then, he would almost wake up, trying to get comfortable on the hard wooden bench, and then sink back into a deep sleep. One morning he awoke just long enough to hear the chanting of the Torah verses from Leviticus 24:5–6 in which God instructs the children of Israel to place twelve loaves of *chalah* on a table in the ancient wilderness tabernacle.

When services ended, the wealthy man woke up, not realizing that all he had heard was the Torah reading about how God wanted twelve loaves of *chalah*. He thought that God had come to him in his sleep and had asked him personally to bring twelve loaves of *chalah* to God. The rich man felt honored that God should single him out, but he also felt a little foolish. Of all the things God could want from a person, twelve loaves of *chalah* did not seem very important. But who was he to argue with God? He went home and baked the bread.

Upon returning to the synagogue, he decided the only proper place for his holy gift was alongside the Torah scrolls in the ark. He carefully arranged the loaves and said to God, "Thank You for telling me what You want of me. Pleasing You makes me very happy." Then he left.

No sooner had he gone than the poorest Jew in the town, the synagogue janitor, entered the sanctuary. All alone, he spoke to God. "O Lord, I am so poor. My family is starving; we have nothing to eat. Unless You perform a miracle for us, we will surely perish." Then, as was his custom, he walked around the room to tidy it up. When he ascended the *bimah* and opened the ark, there before him were twelve loaves of *chalah*! "A miracle!" exclaimed the poor man. "I had no idea You worked so quickly! Blessed are You, O God, who answers our prayers." Then he ran home to share the bread with his family.

Minutes later, the rich man returned to the sanctuary, curious to know whether or not God ate the *chalah*. Slowly he ascended the *bimah*, opened the ark, and saw that the *chalot* were gone. "Oh, my God!" he shouted. "You really ate my *chalot*! I thought You were teasing. This is wonderful. You can be sure that I'll bring another twelve loaves—with raisins in them too!"

The following week, the rich man brought a dozen loaves to the synagogue and again left them in the ark. Minutes later, the poor man entered the sanctuary. "God, I don't know how to say this, but I'm out of food again. Seven loaves we ate, four we sold, and one we gave to charity. But now, nothing is left and, unless You do another miracle, we surely will starve." He approached the ark and slowly opened its doors. "Another miracle!" he cried. "Twelve more loaves, and with raisins too! Thank You God. This is wonderful!"

The *chalah* exchange became a weekly ritual that continued for many years. And, like most rituals that become routine, neither man gave it much thought. Then, one day, the rabbi, detained in the sanctuary longer than usual, watched the rich man place the dozen loaves in the ark and the poor man redeem them.

The rabbi called the two men together and told them what they had been doing.

"I see," said the rich man sadly, "God doesn't really eat *chalah*."

"I understand," said the poor man, "God hasn't been baking *chalah* for me after all."

They both feared that now God no longer would be present in their lives.

Then the rabbi asked them to look at their hands. "Your hands," he said to the rich man, "are the hands of God giving food to the poor. And your hands," said the rabbi to the poor man, "also are the hands of God, receiving gifts from the rich. So you see, God can still be present in your lives. Continue baking and continue taking. Your hands are the hands of God."

The Wilderness of Preparation

THE WILDERNESS IS NOT JUST A DESERT through which we wandered for forty years. It is a way of being. A place that demands being open to the flow of life around you. A place that demands being honest with yourself without regard to the cost in personal anxiety. A place that demands being present with all of yourself.

In the wilderness your possessions cannot surround you. Your preconceptions cannot protect you. Your logic cannot promise you the future. Your guilt can no longer place you safely in the past. You are left alone each day with an immediacy that astonishes, chastens, and exults. You see the world as if for the first time.

Now you might say that the promise of such spiritual awareness could only keep one with the greatest determination in the wilderness but for a moment or so. That such a way of being would be like breathing pure oxygen. We would live our lives in but a few hours and die of old age. "It is better for us to serve the Egyptians than to die in the wilderness." (Exodus 14:12) And indeed, that is your choice.

God in the Midst of Evil

FORGET ABOUT A GOOD PERSON who contracts a terrible disease and dies prematurely or about a wicked one getting rich and living to a ripe old age. Let's go right to the core of the question about evil. Consider a random image from myriad nightmares and agonies human beings have inflicted on one another. It would inevitably come up sooner or later in the conversation anyway and, as it invariably does (and perhaps should), silence further discussion.

There is a wall-size photograph in Yad Va-shem, Israel's memorial to those who perished in the Holocaust. Before us is a great empty field somewhere "in the East." Near the bottom, in the left corner, we see part of a huge (but, for this kind of "action," not atypical) mass grave. The ditch is large enough to contain perhaps a dozen suburban American houses. This freshly dug valley is already partially filled with the naked, bloodied bodies of men, women, young men, young women, little boys, little girls, children, infants. (Lime has been sprinkled on the bodies.) We know from other accounts that they are not all dead. Many in the ditch are merely wounded. We know from written accounts of similar scenes that the mass of corpses and still living bodies moves, bleeds, writhes, and moans. (It was strictly forbidden to take such a photo.)

In the center of the mural, at least as large as the viewer, there are three people: a mother, holding her infant child to her bosom, faces the trench. Just behind her, at point blank range, a young German soldier trains the sights of his rifle at the woman's head, about to shoot. (The end of the rifle barrel is no farther away from her head than the reader's eyes are from this printed page.) In the background there are clouds and the gently waving autumn grass of this unnamed Polish field.

If there is a God, where was that God when this photograph was taken? God was there. See, we have a photograph. There is God, over there in the ditch, in the mother's terrified eyes, even in the psychosis of the Nazi soldier. There is God, an ashen reality, now almost two generations later, more mysterious and holy than ever. The question is not where was God, but why do human beings do such things? Blaming God not only absolves us but increases the likelihood that we will allow such a horror to happen again.

How could God allow such a thing? Why didn't God do anything? To ask such questions assumes that God occasionally intervenes in human affairs without human agency. Yet countless events remind us that God does not work like that. Indeed, while it contradicts literal readings of some sacred texts, we suspect that God never has. God did not die in the Holocaust, only the Deuteronomic idea of a God who rewards and punishes people through suspending laws of nature.

Biblical accounts of earth swallowing villains, seas splitting to save innocents, or wicked nations being blotted out seem now, in the aftermath of the Holocaust, clearly to be metaphors—never meant to be taken literally. If the world of the Bible were so ontologically different from our world today as to permit such divine intervention, then truths from such a time are irrelevant. For us, the snowflakes and rays of sunlight fall without discrimination on righteous and wicked alike. This is simply how the world works. And all theology after the Holocaust must begin with this acknowledgment.

What then is left to talk about? What is evil and where does it come from?

BAD AND EVIL

First of all, many things are bad that are not evil. This is a very important but often overlooked distinction. "Bad" means "unfortunate," "painful," and even "horrible," but it does not mean that someone is necessarily responsible for what has happened. A freak accident, for which no one is to blame, for instance, is "bad" but it is not "evil." Other times, "bad" means "unethical," "wicked," and "evil." We cry out that things should have been otherwise and that someone is to blame. And, if the one who is to blame did so with intention, then the "bad" is also "evil." So "bad" can mean either "unfortunate," as in "no one is to blame," or it can also mean "evil," as in "someone has caused this bad thing to happen."

This double meaning of "bad" probably reflects a time when human beings believed they were powerless in the face of whatever befell them and that everything that happened was caused by God. Indeed, to this day, we still blame God for all sorts of things that are simply "bad" and even for what are entirely human acts. And, of course, when we do, we absolve ourselves of responsibility.

God does not intervene in the affairs of people, at least not in the way a parent might step in to settle a fight between children, take one of them to a physician, judge between righteous and wicked, punish the guilty, reward the righteous. These things can and do occur but only through human agency.

The question therefore "Why is there evil in the world?" means "Why are human beings evil?" or "What is the origin of human cruelty?" Sometimes people suffer because of some evil they themselves or others did or did not do, and sometimes they suffer through no one's fault, although the range of accidents tends to diminish sharply with maturity and responsibility.

If we rule out "accidental" tragedies that could have been prevented had the victim not taken some voluntary risk, we are left with only freak, hopelessly unforeseeable accidents like a tornado or a rare illness. And if we hold our society similarly responsible, for example, for not creating adequate safety measures or directing its energy to the prevention of disease, then the list is even further diminished. How much misery might be prevented, for instance, if humanity chose to allocate its resources toward healing rather than war?

Whenever something bad happens and the guilty ones are too many, too powerful, too distant, or unknown, we blame God. After all, if God runs nature, large undefined parts of history, and anything else we cannot figure out, then the "bad" thing that happened must be the deliberate result of God's intention, an indirect result of God's powerlessness, or God's inexcusable inattention. In other words, whenever we say that some terrible natural event was "bad," and mean it was "evil," then God must either be malevolent or punishing us. We have entered "cosmic bogeyman theology." God has no escape.

Two Universes

Once you acknowledge that bad things happen and that people do evil things, there are only two options: Satan and God. In one universe, people maintain their "selves," their sanity, and God by giving evil its independence. Such wickedness, they reason, could not possibly have anything to do with God. There must be some other non-God power that makes it real, gives it vitality, and with whom God is in eternal conflict. In such a universe, where the source of evil is other than God, sooner or later, one way or another, you wind up with some kind of demonic force, *sitra achra*, Other side, devil, or Satan.

In the second world, God is somehow part of the evil, present even in its depths. This is the meaning of our assertion that "God is One." (Deuteronomy 6:4) A Oneness at the core of all being toward whom everything—yes, everything, even evil—ultimately converges. The source of all reality. If God is the source of all being and human evil is real, then God therefore must be in it also. The evil does not derive its being from some extra-Divine source. This is certainly what Job learns when God speaks to him from out of the whirlwind, God does not cause, tolerate or even forebear the evil, but God, as with everything else in creation, is in it.

It's All God

And if God is everywhere, God is also in the perverse things we plan and even carry out. To be sure, God is less evident and less accessible than in acts of kindness, for example, but in them nevertheless. In the words of Rabbi Tsaddok Hakohen, a student of the school of Mordecai Yosef of Ishbitz, "God is present even in our sins." And rejecting our sins only postpones the ultimate task of healing and self-unification. Accepting our selves is another way of finding God. Dr. David Blumenthal of Emory University offers a similar teaching.

> Evil, in its most profound sense, is contingent upon God for its very existence. There would be no shells [or broken pieces] if there were no sparks... God is everywhere, even in the impulse to rebel against Him. Reality is one. At this point, evil ceases to be grasped as an independent seductive force; it collapses ontologically and falls by the wayside psychologically. One's consciousness is, rather, filled with God.[1]

Aryeh Kaplan, the contemporary philosopher, explains it thus:

> The Baal Shem Tov taught that God is actually hidden within all evil and suffering, but that God only hides when people do not realize that God is there... Ultimately, there is no barrier between God and people except that of our own making, and if one succeeds in removing this barrier, then all evil is revealed to be an illusion.[2]

HUMAN EVIL AND TEARING APART

Why do people occasionally do horrible things? The obvious answer is because human free will, by definition, requires that we be free to choose between good and evil. But this only postpones the deeper problem: Why would anyone ever choose evil at all? Why would a human being ever do anything cruel? That is the question. According to Jewish legend, the pain of being a human being, and for many, the evil they do, originate in two primal, psycho-spiritual "tearings." Something is separated, rejected, and made "other." And the memory of the tearing, the wound, is just too painful to remember.

In the first tearing, a part of ourselves is rejected and identified as "enemy." The second tearing involves every human being's traumatic separation from his or her parents, the process of individuation and of becoming autonomous. Both are lifelong, unending struggles. In one, we tear off a part of ourselves to maintain our own sense of goodness, and in the other, we experience ourselves as having been torn away for our own good. They are both suggested by biblical and subsequent rabbinic legend. And important elements of each are expressed in the story of Jacob's life. Esau is made into an enemy. And Jacob must leave his parents, never to see them again.

AMALEK AND ESAU

In order to understand the first tearing and the process that makes Esau an enemy we must consider the legends surrounding Amalek, the paradigm enemy of the Jewish people. Emerging from the brief wilderness accounts of how, for no apparent reason, he fell upon the weary stragglers at the tail end of the Israelite wanderers, rabbinic tradition imagines that Amalek must be the progenitor of every subsequent enemy of the Jewish people. His very reason for living is to injure Jews. And, according to Deuteronomic injunction, Jews are commanded to blot out his memory for all time. (Deuteronomy 25:17–19) (The commandment is specifically and paradoxically to remember to forget!) The ruthless Haman of the Esther story and the cruelty of Rome are mythically connected through the same malevolent seed: Amalek.

This is not the simple "good guy/bad guy" scenario it first appears to be. The rabbis go on to teach that the wicked Amalek is descended from a woman named Timna. And while Timna was once in love with Jacob, he wouldn't give her the time of day. Thus spurned, she became instead a concubine of Jacob's nephew, Eliphaz.[3] She reasoned, "Since I am not worthy of being Jacob's wife, let me be at least, Eliphaz's handmaid." (*Bereshit Rabba* 82:14) Vindictively bitter over her rejection, she raised her family to hate Jacob and all his progeny, the children of Israel.

This messy family arrangement also means of course that Timna's father-in-law was Jacob's twin, Esau. And rabbinic tradition is quick to note that not only was Esau himself rejected, but that he once even shared a womb with Jacob. Nothing more than the thinness of a membrane separated Esau, the great-grandfather of Amalek, from Jacob!

Why did the Holy One create both the hell of Gehenna and the heaven of the Garden of Eden? In order that one may borrow room from the other. And how much space is there separating them? The rabbis said that they are right next to one another. Not even the thinness of a membrane separated Esau and Jacob. (*Pesikta deRav Kahannah, Shemini Atzeret,* 30)

Jacob rejects Timna, Jacob rejects Esau. They would have loved to be, or once were, part of him. Now they are "other." Now they are enemy. Being torn away, that is the source of the pain and probably of the pain we, in turn, inflict on others. All humanity is a closed organic system. Pain put into the system, sooner or later, comes back to us. Generation after generation. What goes around, comes around.

We now understand why the struggle between Jacob and Esau assumes such significance. That night, over two decades later, when Jacob is left alone on the other side of the Jabok, he wrestles with another being. Was it his conscience, an angel, the patron of Esau, a divine being, or perhaps a once rejected side of himself? The text does say, "You have wrestled with beings divine and human..." (Genesis 32:29)

This possibility that the nocturnal battle involved God is born out in another constellation of legends. The Talmud imagines that the dust from their wrestling ascended all the way to the Throne of Glory itself. (*Hullin* 91a)

Rabbi Joshua ben Levi explained it this way: Since the same word is used in both Genesis 32:26, "As he wrestled *(b'hay-avko)* with him," referring to the struggle, and in Nahum 1:3, "...And the clouds are the dust *(avak)* of God's feet," alluding to the Throne of Glory, we may conclude that dust from their wrestling rose all the way to God.

Or, as Rabbi Aryeh Leib of Ger explains, since the form of Jacob is engraved on the Throne of Glory, then the effects of any earthly struggle with the Other Side also must affect the Throne on High.[4] The battle is not between us and some independent power. The struggle goes on inside God. It is part of God; it is part of ourselves. But the struggle is not against anything intrinsically evil. (Indeed, nothing *is* intrinsically evil.) This means that God somehow must be connected with Esau, the source of Amalek, the great-grandparent of all our enemies.

The unnamed night wrestler of Genesis 32 represents a dimension of ourselves that has been rejected and labeled as "evil other." It comes back to injure and name us during the night. And since it is still a part of ourselves we cannot bear to acknowledge, when we sense it in someone else, we are all the more frightened and angry.

And often, failing to find it in someone else, we project it onto them anyway, for this deludes and comforts us into feeling that we have utterly torn it away. Hating something in someone else is easier than self-reproach.

Once we realize that what we detest in another person only wants to be accepted, taken back, and loved, do we begin to diminish our own capacity for evil. By embracing what was never really other, we neutralize the evil. We heal and redeem it and in so doing we heal ourselves and God.

One final image may be helpful in understanding how what has been torn away can be redeemed. Early Hasidism developed a doctrine called "strange thoughts," or "lascivious thoughts during prayer." According to this teaching, one sure sign that we have attained a high level in prayer is that invariably we will be assailed by embarrassingly wicked thoughts. Our first inclination is to reject them at once, but, as everyone knows, this only gives them even greater power over our prayers. We must, counsels the Baal Shem, realize that such thoughts are in reality only rejected parts of ourselves that sense this time of great closeness to God and come out of our unconscious, yearning for redemption. As Yakov Yosef of Polnoye, a student of the Baal Shem Tov, used to teach his students:

> One must believe that "the whole world is filled with [God's] presence" (Isaiah 6:3) and [as we learn from *Tikkunei Zohar*] that "there is no place empty of [God]." All human thoughts have within them the reality of God.... When a strange or evil thought arises in a person's mind while he is engaged in prayer, it is coming to that person to be repaired and elevated.[5]

The goal, as the Hasidim say, is to "...find the root of love in evil so as to sweeten evil and turn it into love."[6]

The second form of tearing that is responsible for human evil comes from parents and children separating from one another. The price a human being pays for growing into an autonomous adult is the pain of leaving home. I am now convinced the Eden story intuits this.

If God didn't want Adam and Eve to eat fruit from the tree in the center of the garden, then why put it right there, out in the middle of the garden where Adam and Eve could reach it? Why didn't God just hide the fruit somewhere deep in the forest? And then, equally puzzling, after putting the tree right there in the middle of the garden, why did God specifically tell Adam and Eve to be sure not to eat the fruit?

What a different world it would be if the forbidden fruit were on one unknown random tree hidden deep in some primordial garden. The chances are high that we might never have discovered it. We would all live in childhood eternal.

There is one rabbinic tradition that tells of God's creating other worlds and destroying them before our present universe. Each one was presumably deficient in some vital way. For all we know, God did try creating a world without the tree temptingly planted right in the middle of the garden. Or maybe there was a prior universe in which God neglected to forbid human beings to eat the fruit. Maybe God realized that Adam and Eve weren't clever enough on their own to figure out how to sin. After universes of infantile obedience, they remained tediously, predictably, and incorrigibly infantile.

"Yes, Daddy. Yes, Mommy. Whatever you want."

"This will never work," reasons God. "Better they should know some sin, estrangement, and guilt but at least become autonomous human beings rather than remain these insipid, goody-two-shoes infants. But I can't just make them autonomous. If I did, their autonomy, their individuation, their independence would be a sham. They must earn it themselves. They must want it badly enough to pay a price. I'll let them make their own children, but first they must earn their autonomy."

I suspect it was for this reason, out of desperation, that God resorted to a "setup" that has come to be known as the expulsion from the garden of Eden. Eating the first fruit was not a sin but a necessary, prearranged passage toward human maturity. We have read it all wrong: God was not angry. God rejoiced at our disobedience and then wept with joy that we could feel our estrangement and want to return home.

What Adam and Eve did in the garden of Eden was not a sin. It is what was supposed to happen. Indeed it has happened in every generation since. Children disobey their parents and, in so doing, complete their own creation. Adam and Eve are duped, not by the snake, but by God. They were lovingly tricked into committing the primal act of disobedience that alone could ensure their separation from God, their individuation, and their expulsion from (childhood's) garden. Yet just because such is the way of the world does not mean there is no psychic damage.

The price of autonomy, individuation, is the trauma of separation from parents. At the core of every psyche lies a deep pain. We are not guilty because of Adam and Eve's sin, as in orthodox Christianity's doctrine of original sin. Nor are we sinful as Adam and Eve were sinful, as in Judaism's teaching. For our own good we have been tricked into leaving our parents' home, from separating from God. The issue is not sin, guilt, or even disobedience. The necessary price for becoming an autonomous adult is the unending pain of separation.

To Sweeten the Evil in Yourself

We go down into ourselves with a flashlight—looking for the evil we have intended or done—not to excise it as some alien growth, but rather to discover the holy spark within it. We begin not by rejecting the evil but by acknowledging it as something we meant to do. This is the only way we can truly raise and redeem it.

We lose our temper because we want things to be better right away. We gaze with lustful eyes because we have forgotten how to love the ones we want to love. We hoard material possessions because we imagine they will help us live more fully. We turn a deaf ear, for we fear the pain of listening would kill us. We waste time, because we are not sure how to enter a living relationship. We even tolerate a society that murders, because we are convinced it is the best way to save more life. At the bottom of such behavior is something that was once holy. And during times of holiness, communion, and light our personal and collective perversions creep out of the cellar, begging to be healed, freed, and redeemed.

Rabbi Yakov Yosef of Polnoye, one of the first students of the Baal Shem Tov, taught:

> The essence of the finest *teshuva* [the purest returning to one's Source in Heaven] is that "deliberate sins are transformed into merits," for one turns evil into good, as I heard from my teacher [the Baal Shem Tov], who interpreted the "Turn aside from evil and do good" (Psalm 34:15) to mean: "Turn the evil into good."[7]

The conclusion of true *teshuva*, returning to our Source in Heaven, is not self-rejection or remorse but the healing that comes from telling ourselves the truth about our real intentions and, finally, self-acceptance. Not satisfaction or complacency; it does not mean that we are now proud of who we were or what we did, but it does mean that we have taken what we did back into ourselves, acknowledged it as part of ourselves. We have found its original motive, realized how it became disfigured, perhaps beyond recognition, made real apologies, done our best to repair the injury, but we no longer try to reject who we have been and therefore who we are, for even that is an expression of the Holy One of Being.

We do not simply repudiate the evil we have done and sincerely mean never to do again; that is easy (we do it all the time). We receive whatever evils we have intended and done back into ourselves as our own deliberate creations. We cherish them as long-banished children finally taken home again. And thereby transform them and ourselves. When we say the *vidui*, the confession, on Yom Kippur, we don't hit ourselves. We hold ourselves.

THE TRUTH OF A NAME

"And [Isaac] asked, '…Which of my sons are you?' And Jacob answered his father, 'I am Esau…'" (Genesis 27:18–19)

"Asked the [unnamed night wrestler], 'What is your name?' And [Jacob] replied, 'Jacob.' Whereupon the nameless one responded, 'Your name shall no longer be Jacob, but Israel…'" (Genesis 32:28–29)

This time Jacob tells the truth! Now, over two decades later, he manages to unify both sides of his personality. And the minute he tells the truth about his identity to the nameless night wrestler, his other side, his twin brother, (God?), he is transformed into Israel. Now he is a being who has struggled with beings human and divine and survived. He rises to his destiny.

Bats

I never saw a bat. I hope I never do. One nearly killed a close friend of mine. While he was on a ladder, cleaning a third floor gutter, a bat surprised him. He reflexively jumped backward and landed in a hospital bed for six months.

"That damn bat changed my life," he said. "Gave me all kinds of time to read and just think about what was important. That's when I decided to get involved in the synagogue."

That's how he wound up being chairman of the Rabbi Search Committee. The whole thing makes you wonder. You have some things planned out, but no matter how single-minded you are, other things get mixed in. Things just seem to fly into what you're doing and all you can do is hang on for dear life. Take how I wound up being the rabbi of a congregation in suburban Boston for the past quarter century.

I was about to complete a two-year rabbinic fellowship near Chicago. Karen and I knew only that we hoped to find a small congregation somewhere in the Northeast. I managed to get three interviews: one in Montreal, one on Long Island, one west of Boston. I bought a new suit, went to the barber, and got on an airplane. I thought Montreal and Long Island were okay, but they didn't think I was. The third congregation, only a few years old, had already been ravaged by several power struggles over phony religious issues. Colleagues in the area warned me to stay away: "It's a mess."

During the interview, the members of the search committee spent most of their time yelling at one another. When they finished, they started on the young man in the new suit. Believing that the best defense was a good offense, I remember suggesting that a decent rabbi would make it hard for them to go on pretending that they were just another Protestant denomination in a Yankee town. That got their attention. There was more yelling and shouting. The interview ended abruptly with an embarrassed silence.

When I phoned Karen afterward, I didn't even bother going into details: "Forget it, honey. No way is this one gonna happen. Too bad, the chairman is really a beautiful man. It'd be great to work with him, but it wasn't meant to be."

He was an amazing man. For a living, he joked to me years later, he sold the government high-tech hardware they didn't really need, so it was relatively easy to sell the congregation a rabbi they didn't really want. When he met me at the airport, during the long ride to the interview, he had made up his mind that I was the rabbi he was looking for. So he drove me on a detour around a much more beautiful, neighboring town and told me that was where the congregation was. He convinced me it would be the opportunity of a lifetime: "People here can go in any direction." He must have done some job on the committee too, because they called me back for a second chance.

This time the discussion was more civil, even polite. It was as if they had never met me before. The chairman led the discussion with great tact and diplomacy. It wasn't until over a decade later that I realized just how much diplomacy. After a few years of my rabbinic leadership, all but three of the original members on the search committee had resigned from the congregation. But miraculously, I still had a job.

Over the years, my friend and I bicycled together and talked politics. I performed the *b'nai mitzvah* of his children. It's been over a decade since he died of cancer. To conduct the funeral of a dear friend, someone so influential in your life, is a sacred honor. I was scheduled to go to Israel when he entered the final stages of the terrible disease. His family and I agreed that if he should die while I was gone, I would return for the funeral. I visited his silent bedside the day before I left. He was on painkillers and barely conscious.

Still, I fantasized he might understand what I was saying, but there was no way to be certain. "Thank you for touching my life. If I have failed you or hurt you, please forgive me. I love you."

A week later, upon returning from Israel, I learned that there had been no change. The hospital room was serene in the dim light. I approached the bed almost reverently, but before I could say anything, the unconscious man in the bed before us suddenly sat straight up. We all jumped back. He stared at us as if he were trying to see, then slowly eased himself down. He said nothing.

"I've never seen anything like it," whispered his nurse. "After such a long span of inaction, to have such energy. Do you suppose he was trying to say goodbye?"

It's funny how people pop into our lives. Often, we don't realize the role they played until long after they've gone. Perhaps it's just as well. If we knew who they'd turn out to be, we might run away or step backward off a ladder.

Most of us believe in free will. Most of us however also have known moments when we felt as if we were permitted to survey our lives from such a high vantage point that our freedom was revealed to be illusory. The closer we are to what is happening, the more we believe we are in complete control. The farther away we get, the more we are willing to acknowledge the participation of something greater. We realize that we were part of something much larger than our daily decisions.

Everything is organically, seamlessly joined to everything else. We have been players in a divine scheme, neither marionettes nor zombies but waves in an ocean, dancers in a ballet, colors on a canvas, words in a story. Discrete and probably autonomous, but never entirely independent. Of course, it is preposterous. Of course, it makes no rational sense. But for just a moment, it is as if we encounter our destiny. Everything is *within* God.

This does not mean that we give in and simply "go with the flow." Indeed, what is "set before us" to accomplish frequently requires stubborn, solitary, courageous, and "seemingly" voluntary action. But now what we do feels less fragmented than before. Now we understand the strange Talmudic maxim: "All is in the hands of heaven, except the fear of heaven." The only thing truly within our power, and our power alone, may be whether or not we will behave in each moment with arrogance or reverence. Other than that, life goes on as before. The only difference is that now we do what we do with reverence. "In life, unlike in literature," as Professor Uriel Simon of Bar Ilan University has taught, "we cannot always discern the hand of God."

Heaven has assigned a role to each of us. It's the only one we're going to get. Sometimes we don't like our part. We want someone else's lines, costume, entrance. I, for instance, think I should have been assigned the role of starting quarterback for the San Francisco '49ers.

"Sorry, that part's taken. You get to be the rabbi in a small town in Massachusetts. That's the only part we've got for you. You want it or not?"

If we say, "O.K., I'll take the part. I choose to play it with all my strength," then, even though we probably won't make it into the National Football League, it won't matter. We wouldn't take the job even if they coaxed us because we'll be having too much fun being who we are. But if, on the other hand, we sulk or stubbornly try to seize some other actor's part by pretending we're someone else, then we just wind up being a second-rate actor in a "B" movie of our life story.

I counsel my students on the eve of their graduation from rabbinic school, all terrified that they won't get the job they want: "Relax, because God is going to put you where God wants you—whether you like it or not."

Everyone and everything moves within the divine. Even bats.

A House of Cardboard

In New York City, on Fifty-fifth Street, just off Madison Avenue, I passed a man who seemed to be living in a big cardboard box. It probably originally protected a major appliance that was delivered to one of the town houses or condos in the neighborhood. Those places go for hundreds of thousands, even millions of dollars.

I didn't want to be nosy, but as far as I could tell the man kept most of his possessions in a broken shopping cart. At night, it starts to get chilly this time of year, so he had carefully erected his home over a grate in the sidewalk to catch the heat. He had to do this because his "home" had no utilities. He might have been one of the ambulatory schizophrenics that have been put out on the streets with the city's budget cuts. Maybe he was just a failure and had no family to help him out.

But one thing was clear: This was his home. Since it could be interpreted as a "permanent dwelling," Jewish law would require that a *mezzuzah* be affixed to the doorframe. Obviously it would have been tricky to do that even if we could be sure where the door was.

I was struck by how nonchalant I felt as I looked into the door (or maybe it was the window) of this man's home, as if I were noting an interesting automobile parked at the curb or a clever shop window display, without paying full attention. Just another ordinary city street scene: a man living off Madison Avenue in a cardboard box. I am ashamed that I was numb to such a sight.

And Jews wonder why God commands us to leave our $100,000, $250,000, $750,000 condos and apartments and homes for one week during the festival of *Sukkot* and live in a booth, a hut, a *sukka*, with no more roof over our heads than what we find laying in the woods. It's not that we should be grateful that we don't have to live like this all year but that we be humbled because a whole lot of folks nearby really do.

4

Creation's Blueprint

Tolstoy once observed that the closer you are to an event the more you imagine you have some control over it. He also said that the farther away you get from an event, the more you realize that it was part of something bigger than you. That might explain why young people think they can change things, while old people are content to spend more time watching (and learning from) what is going on.

Think of it this way: Either some things are connected to one another, in which case, everything is connected to everything else and therefore filled with potential meaning. Or nothing is connected to anything, in which case existence is a crapshoot. The former approach is a roundabout way of saying there is a God, the latter approach, that existence is pointless and absurd.

The Baal Shem Tov tells of how a man "wears out his shoes" traveling to a faraway land on what he thinks is a business trip. The real reason for the journey was so that he could eat a particular piece of bread that was waiting for him there. It may well happen that the trip does not even concern him but instead one of his servants. If there is a piece of bread or a glass of water the servant needs to consume, and if he cannot make the journey to that place on his own, then the servant's master is influenced by something else to make the journey and enable his servant to eat that bread or drink that water tha was pre-ordained for him. But people do not think this way. On the contrary, they merely proceed on their journeys, while their hearts are oblivious that it is all from God.

In this way the Baal Shem Tov teaches that with or without our consent or knowledge, we live within one great system of mutual interdependence and meaning. And the true expression of our autonomy is explained in the cryptic passage found in tractate *Berakhot* 33b, "Everything is in the hands of Heaven except whether or not you are reverent."

According to mystical Jewish tradition, the master blueprint for just how everything is interconnected is the scroll of the Torah. It is what God drew up before God began the creation as a kind of blueprint. And one who studies Torah, therefore, is studying the DNA of being itself.

The Letter Kof

THE BOTTOM OF THE *KOF* IS MAN CALLING "HOLY" so that he can join himself to his Creator. The top line, sheltering and reaching down, is the Holy One.

Kof is the voice of an angel calling, "*Kadosh, kadosh, kadosh*, Holy, holy, holy is the Lord of Hosts."

Kof is the voice, *kol*, of a person proclaiming the oneness of God. *K'ri-at Shema*. And the holiness of God, *kaddish*. And the holiness of a *Shabbat* or of a festival, *kiddush*. And the holiness of a spouse, *kiddushin*. *Kof* is the voice of holiness.

Nothing can be holy without the voice of *kof* to say it is. But remember also that with your voice you can make the whole world holy, *kadosh*.

Kof is one of the letters made by two marks. *Hay* is the other. The lower mark of the *kof* is man calling God. But God also calls man. With the upper mark of the *kof*, God whispers very softly to see if you are really listening: *kol d'mama daka*. A voice that is still and small. A little girl. The daughter of a voice, God's voice, *bat kol*. Like an echo. Always listen.

Such is *kof*. The voice by which man allows God to be present by calling: Holy, *kadosh*. And the voice by which God asks if man wants God to be.

"Holy, holy, holy is the Lord of Hosts. The fullness of the whole earth is His glory."

When Life Is a Story

ELIE WIESEL ONCE SUGGESTED that not everything that happened is true, nor did everything that is true necessarily happen.

Sometimes stories can be true without ever having happened. The story of the garden of Eden, for instance, obviously never happened the way it is told. Snakes don't talk, fruit doesn't contain the secret of life, and people don't wear clothing made from fig leaves.

But the story is *true*. In metaphoric language, to be sure, the legend describes a drama that occurs in the lifetime of every human being. We are not guilty because Adam and Eve were; but we are guilty in precisely the same way. The story is true not because it happened, but because it happens generation after generation. That's why we keep reading it.

The stories that describe the events of our lives are true insofar as they resemble the great archetypic myths. The best movies help us imagine the archetype. Movies are box office hits because they manage (like all great art, often despite the conscious designs of their creators) to portray a mythic truth. When a life experience replicates the great story, we often surprise ourselves by saying, "Wow, my life here is so real, it resembles a movie!" And conversely, movies strike us as true beyond their stories when they seem to capture something of the truth that lies beneath the surface of all creation. This is what we mean when we say that scripture is holy: it speaks the truth beneath the surface. Indeed, the literal text is only a mechanism. As the rabbis used to say, the Bible could not merely be the stories it tells, for we could easily tell better stories!

All the great moments of our lives transcend our lives. We cease to be autonomous actors and find ourselves "taken over" by some ancient script. The bride and the groom who marshal all their energies to fashion a creative wedding are, in the last analysis, only Adam and Eve all over again. Indeed, to the extent that they are able to permit the great myth to guide their actions and words will their wedding be complete. We give ourselves over to the Great Story, allow ourselves to be carried along by its universal truth. We taste eternity.

The Blueprint inside Creation

BLUEPRINTS ARE WRITTEN INSTRUCTIONS for constructing a building. They show the design of the completed structure that forever remains within the building. In the same way, sheet music instructs the musician. The notes are on paper, but whenever the melody is played, they are also in the music. If you have ever tried to build a complicated model or play a song on the piano, you understand why it is important to have a plan before you begin.

Scientists have discovered that each person has within every cell of his or her body a tiny molecule called DNA, which contains a genetic code. It is a personal blueprint, a plan for his or her body— the color of one's eyes, the shape of one's face, and even how tall one will grow. Our universe also has such a plan.

At the beginning of the beginning, God was unable to create the world. No matter how many times and how many different ways God tried to arrange them, the parts wouldn't fit together. The universe kept collapsing because God had no diagram, no design.

God said, "I need an overall plan for My world. I want it to be One, as I am One... I know what I will do, I will use Torah as a blueprint for creation and that way all the parts of the world will fit together, and I and My Torah will be inside everything!"

Long ago, our rabbis understood this. When we read in the Book of Proverbs (8:22) that "God made me as the very first thing," the rabbis understood "me" to mean that the Torah preceded creation. They did not mean the *sefer Torah* we keep in the ark but an idea or a plan that God could use. They discovered this same idea when they realized that there were two ways to translate *b'ray-sheet*, the first Hebrew word in the Book of Genesis.

We usually translate *b'ray-sheet* as "In the beginning." But the rabbis noticed that the Hebrew letter *beit* doesn't always mean "in"; it can also mean "with." If that is so, then *b'ray-sheet* (as in "In the beginning God created the heavens and the earth") also could be saying, "With *ray-sheet* God created the heavens and the earth." And this would mean, suggested the rabbis, that *ray-sheet* must be another name for Torah. In other words, God created the world with Torah. Torah is God's blueprint for the world. (*Bereshit Rabba* 1:1)

One rabbinic legend says that the words of Torah are spoken continuously from Mount Sinai without interruption. (*Pirke Avot* 6:2; *Shemot Rabba* 41:7) We cannot hear the voice because of the noise and distractions all around us. Even when we shut off the television and ask everyone in the room to be silent, even when we stop making sounds ourselves, there is still the distracting "noise" of thinking going on inside our own heads. And that is what made Mount Sinai so special: God hushed the world to perfect silence.

When God gave the Torah, no bird chirped and no fowl flew, the wind and sea stood still, and the angels stopped singing, "Holy, holy, holy." Once there was complete silence, God's voice went forth. (*Shemot Rabba* 29:9) And everyone could hear the words of Torah that had been there all along.

The Body of the Universe

THE HISTORY OF HUMANITY might have been the life span of one man. Once there was only one person in the universe: *Adam HaRishon,* the first man. And this man had but one commandment: Thou shall not eat of the tree. How simple it all might have been had this Adam man not had such an uncontrollable hunger for eating knowledge-fruit from the tree. If only he could have held out long enough to satisfy the Creator that our world experiment was a success.

There is a legend (which I once heard from Rabbi Shelly Gordon, may his memory be for a blessing) that concerns itself with just this same possibility. If the first Adam-man had fulfilled the only—and also, therefore, every commandment there was—might we not assume that there would have been no reason to expel him from the garden. No need to populate the world. No need for all the commandments and their transgressions. No need for world history. What if the Creator only intended that there be one person and not teeming billions. And that that one person fulfill only one commandment.

Was not the first Adam-man perhaps created on the eve of the seventh day and given one commandment with the divine hope that he could restrain his unrestrainable hunger for but one span of twenty-four hours? For then the creation venture might have been concluded a prompt success. One man. One commandment. One Sabbath. The first man would have been also the last man. The Adam-man would also have been the Messiah.

Now it is true that this tale enables us to imagine the beginning and the end within one sentence. Within the life span of one person. Whatever it was that happened to mankind happened to the first Adam-man during his one Sabbath-day-long life. One and the same life-force-awareness unites all human history. Couples the beginning with the end.

There is a contemporary legend that was first told by Arthur Clarke and visualized by Stanley Kubrick in *2001* that also tries to unite the beginning and the end. Once, so the tale goes, our planet was visited by some supremely intelligent, beneficent, and curious alien. This visitor noticed that one ape seemed to be fascinated by the moon. All the others were too busy staying alive to have time for such wonderment. The visitor decided to show the moon-watcher how to extend his hand by using a simple tool. And in so doing initiated what has come to be known as human history and, incidentally, the visitor's own claim to deity. But since this visiting creator had other galaxies to explore, he devised a clever scheme whereby he might learn if his experiment would succeed. He planted some kind of cosmic alarm clock on the moon that was set to go off the moment his protégé, the moon-watching man-ape should discover it. For surely if he could rise above his fellow animals enough to reach the moon, then it would be worth the creator's time to return for a reunion.

For all these aeons of humanity, the tale suggests, we have been watched. Our progress and ascent have been hoped for. Somewhere at the furthest reaches of the cosmos there waits someone for some ape-man-child-astronaut-explorer for what will be surely the greatest reunion of them all. Standing there in space the first visitor-creator will welcome the last man-explorer. He will say something like, "So we meet again. I was not sure there for a long time whether you would ever make it. But you have and my experiment has been a success."

Now this tale, despite its substitution for the ancient Holy One (whom religious people call God) with some space man is also about creation and redemption. Our existence is an experiment.

Our redemption is the result of some accomplishment. The end and the beginning are joined by some common purpose. And here too, one and the same life-force awareness unites all human history. Of course here the unity resides in the life of the first visitor-creator/the last visited-redeemer.

Or does it? What if there is as much unity in the countless generations separating the first man-ape and the last man-child-astronaut-explorer as there is in the single seemingly infinite life span of the cosmic visitor? What if all life is really the same life? What if what we call the end of our individual lives is only an illusion? Suppose we, each of us, are as much a part of those who precede and follow us as our childhood is of our old age? And that like some life disconnected and interrupted by flashes of amnesia, which is, nevertheless the same life, so too with the generations of human history. I cannot remember personally being freed from Egypt but nevertheless I *myself* was freed from Egypt.

There is another Kabbalistic legend that tells of all humankind descending from another Adam. *Adam Kadmon*, the primordial archetypic man, which the Kabbala is careful to distinguish from *Adam Ha-Rishon*, the first mythic man of the garden, lest the distinction between man and God be confused. But by allowing them both to share the name "Adam" the blasphemous-holy confusion is nevertheless intimated. This primordial Adam was some kind of giant who contained within him the souls of us all. After the Fall they were scattered about the universe like sparks. They are never extinguished. There are only so many of them. They are each an eternal life force that gives life to one creature after another in one generation after another. And each of them began in the same *Adam Kadmon*, the same archetypic man, the same primordial giant. And at the end, they will return once again to their same ancient unity.

Perhaps in some other galaxy it is the way of life to continue from childhood to adolescence to maturity to old age without interruption or forgetting. Life awareness and continuity might span what we see as generations. But for us of this world, the continuity of lifetimes seem irreparably severed by death and inexplicably initiated by birth. Those life-sustaining sparks scattered from *Adam Kadmon* do not seem to be linked from one generation to the next. Somehow our consciousness of our journey is stricken with amnesia.

"Everybody carries the secret trace of the transmigrations of his soul in the lineaments of his forehead and his hands, and in the aura which radiates from his body."[1]

It is said of the holy ones of old that they could look onto a forehead and see to the very depths of a soul. See all its travels and affairs. Transmigrations and incarnations. All its folly and all its holiness. All the way back to its origin on one of the limbs of the first man himself. All the way back to the very root of its existence. All of which grew from one and the same tree.

"Rabbi Simeon ben Lakish said in the name of Rabbi Eleazar ben Azariah: At the time that the Holy One, blessed be He, was creating Adam, He had come to the stage in creating him when Adam had the form of a golem, an unarticulated embryo, which lay prone from one end of the world to the other. Then the Holy One, blessed be He, caused to pass before the golem each generation with its righteous men, each generation with its wicked men, each generation with its scholars, each generation with its leaders..." (*Pesikta Rabbati* 23:1) And this primordial archetype being is recreated in each embryo, which likewise is permitted to see from one end to the other.

But it is the same thing whether you start at the beginning and understand how Adam foresaw and contained all those yet to issue from him. Or whether you look into your own forehead and follow yourself all the way back to the first man. (Or before and through him to the Holy One Himself.)

If light is awareness, then creation stories, beginning with light, are man telling about himself. Ink blots from some long ago present. Mirrors in which we might see back through the adolescent sophistication of which we are so proud.

Once we tried to pluck out our eyes in a vain attempt at objectivity. Then we learned that some subjectivity is inescapable. As Heisenberg discovered: to observe is to participate. We change what we look at simply by looking at it. So we left our eyes in our heads. Now we are being coaxed to look at one's eyes themselves. For the thinker is thinking about himself.

Our drive to find the light hidden long ago can only lead us back to an awareness of ourselves.

There are two directions of astonishment. Here is how it happens. Above us arches the immensity of the heavens. That if the thickness of this page of paper were to equal the 93 million miles between the earth and the sun then the distance to the edge of the known universe would be a stack of papers 31 million miles high.

And within us breathes the intricacy of our bodies. That in each of the 100 trillion cells of every human body, there are roughly 100,000 genes coiled on a molecule of deoxyribonucleic acid, which if uncoiled and unwound would string back and forth between the earth and the sun over 400 times.

Human beings stand at the center of these two infinite directions. Above us space and time are literally astronomic. Within us space and time are infinitesimal. And now we understand that the universe is expanding. Growing ever larger. And that with each new microscope the inner biology grows ever smaller. In a word: we will never see the farthest thing above nor the smallest thing within. The greatness of the distance and the minuteness of the size will always increase simultaneously. It is almost as if we were driven to maintain this balance that always leaves us in the center.

Adam Ha-Rishon, the first man and the last man are one and the same. The one who left the garden in order to continue eating from knowledge will, after all the generations have come and gone, at long last be sated. Even as he will be the same one who will be called God's anointed one. The Messiah who will return to the garden.

If we had remained in Eden we would have been as one with the universe. But we never could have been conscious of our unity. So we left seeking that unity and consciousness. Leaving the garden is a metaphor for forgetting that we are one with the universe. Holy awareness is the only way to return.

Originally published in *Learn Torah With...*, Torah Aura Productions, 1994

"Not You, but God"

THE JOSEPH "NOVELLA" in the concluding chapters of Genesis may be the first modern story: God in this tale (apparently) does nothing. Throughout the preceding hero narratives and the subsequent national miracle legends of Exodus, God is everywhere, telling people what to do, intervening in their affairs, suspending the laws of nature, klutzing up the plot. But from Genesis 37 until the end of Genesis at chapter 50, God seems to be nowhere. God talks to no one, apparently lets folks do pretty much whatever they please, tolerates the caprice of natural law. The emotional zenith of the story comes when the secret is given. Indeed, only Joseph figures it out. He even tells everyone but they, like most of us, are too caught up in the drama to realize what, as the kids say, "is coming down."

If we switch to a wide-angle lens, we realize that the Joseph saga functions as a kind of transition piece that joins Genesis with Exodus. Its job is to get us down to Egypt. At the beginning of the novella when Jacob gives Joseph that beautiful multi-colored coat, the Jews are a bunch of recalcitrant nomads living in the promised land and in daily communication with God. By the first chapter of Exodus, they have become an enslaved nation of 600,000 souls, living in exile, who haven't had so much as a postcard from God in 400 years! Something seems to have happened.

What has happened is "Joseph"—his agonizing descent into Egypt, his astonishing rise to power, his reconciliation with his family, and finally their subsequent resettlement in Goshen. The characters in the tale are so consumed with trying to manipulate their fortunes that they all (like most of us) fail to notice what is really happening not only around them but—and here is the key idea—through them and despite them. *Nobody* gets it. Nobody but Joseph.

He even tells everyone but they are too preoccupied to appreciate his discovery.

All the players remain stuck in their own convictions that no one is running anything but themselves. Joseph's brothers think they can get away with either killing or selling him. Reuben figures he can outwit them. Judah figures he can skip town without penalty. Potiphar's wife thinks she can have or destroy whomever she pleases. Even Joseph has been trying to manipulate his whole family. All of them are all busy trying to manipulate the outcome of this (apparently) Godless plot—and they are all dumbfounded. Finally, Joseph figures it out.

Sitting up there on his throne, Joseph watches his brothers, remembers his dreams and his father's dotage, Mrs. Potiphar, the dungeon. He listens as Judah "draws near," and realizes that something else has been going on all along. Suddenly, the whole thing is clear: "It was not you," he tells them, "who sent me here but God!" He, in effect, says, "This is just the way things were meant to be from the very beginning. Now I understand that everything to be just the way God had intended it all along. It's all been set up." But what could this mean?

God is to the world as our unconscious is to our everyday lives—quietly, invisibly, secretly guiding our steps; feeding us our lines; moving us into position; unifying everything we do. We are chastened to realize that what we thought was an accident was, in truth, the hand of God. Most of the time we are simply unaware. Awareness takes too much effort, and besides, it's more fun to pretend we are running the show. But every now and then we understand, for just a moment, that God has all along been involved in everything. As Rabbi Zaddok HaKohen of Lublin taught, "The first premise of faith is to believe with perfect faith that there is no such thing as happenstance....Every detail, small or great, they are all from the Holy One." Everything is organically, seamlessly joined to everything else and run by God—or perhaps, simply *is* God.

Nowadays, the sacred usually masquerades as "coincidence." We become aware of some greater network of which we suddenly seem to have always been a part all along. We glimpse at why we were created. The coincidences can take myriad forms. We can have the strange sensation of knowing why we were where we were years ago. We can suddenly sense a presence that binds us to others. Or, we can simply be shocked to discover that what we have been doing fits into some larger purpose. Coincidence is God's way of remaining anonymous.

The Hasidic master, Menachem Mendl of Kotzk, offered the following deliberate "misreading" of another verse near the end of the Joseph story. After having revealed his identity to his brothers and learning that his father was still alive, Joseph dispatches them to Canaan to fetch the old man. The text says, "And as they left he said to them, 'Don't quarrel on the way.'" The Hebrew for "on the way" is *ba-derekh*. But the preposition *ba*, in addition to meaning "on," can also mean "with." "For this reason Joseph said to them," suggests Kotzk, "'the hour of your arrival at your destination has been appointed by Heaven. If you hurry on the way, you will only be delayed by some other reason. So don't quarrel *with* the way that has been appointed for you.'"!

This does not mean that we give in and simply "go with the flow." Indeed, frequently, what is "set before us" to accomplish requires stubborn, solitary, courageous, and "seemingly" autonomous action. But now what we do feels less fragmented than before. Now we understand the strange Talmudic maxim in *Berakhot* 33b: "All is in the hands of Heaven, save the fear of Heaven." The only thing truly within our power, and our power alone, is whether or not we will behave each moment with arrogance or reverence. Beyond that life goes on as before. The only difference is that now we do what we do with *yirat shamayim*, which I would translate as "grateful reverence" or perhaps even "amazing grace."

In this way, we begin to resolve the paradox created by our insistence that God not be allowed in the plot and our fleeting religious hunch that God may actually be running everything. In the final analysis, *that* may be the only difference between life and literature. For "in life," as Professor Uriel Simon of Bar Ilan University has taught, "unlike in literature, we cannot discern the hand of God." And it was Joseph who taught his family and any one else who cares to listen: "It was not you who sent me here but the Holy One!"

Wool Pants

WHEN I WAS A LITTLE BOY GROWING UP IN DETROIT, my family attended a big cathedral of a Reform temple. The sunlight streamed in through the stained glass windows, there were more light bulbs in the chandeliers than stars in the sky, and you could actually feel the organ music with your whole body. We used to tease the organist, a friend of our family's, that he played too loud and nicknamed him "Thunder Foot."

On the Jewish New Year, no matter how early my parents and my brother and I arrived in the main sanctuary, or, as we called it, the "Big Room," my grandfather was always there waiting for us. (This was especially surprising to me because we had driven him there in our car.) There he sat like a proper German gentleman, second aisle on the right, fourth row. There weren't assigned pews, but we always sat there: It was *our* place.

Everyone was all dressed up. My aunt called it *fapitzed,* which meant, I think, wearing more expensive clothes than my aunt could afford. It seemed very important to see everyone and to be seen by everyone. In fact, the main thing everyone seemed to care about was that a lot of people would see what they were wearing. It wasn't one of religion's most sublime expressions, but something sacred was going on.

Every few years, I would get a new outfit for temple. As far as I can tell, it always had wool pants, which seemed to have two properties. First, each trouser leg had a crease down the middle and, if I wasn't careful when I sat down, the crease would disappear at the knee and my mother would get mad at me. The other thing about wool pants was that they all seemed to be made with thousands of perspiration-activated, microscopic needles. This meant that as soon as it got hot, they itched and the boy couldn't sit still. The creases would start to disappear. And then my mother would yell at me. (When I got older, an allergist informed me that I was mildly allergic to wool. So it goes.)

Every year, I would complain, "Ma, what's the big deal about what I'm wearing? I don't care what your friends think I look like." But every year we would go to temple where my brother and I would be inspected by every Jew in Michigan, all of whom seemed to know my parents and cared that my wool pants were neatly creased.

"My, how he's grown," one would sigh.

"What a lovely outfit. Where did you find it?" approved another.

"My pants itch!" I would murmur.

"Stand still!"

With the advent of polyester and a half dozen years, my complaint matured into an adolescent disgust with facade, which, I now suspect, may be the first glimmer of religious maturity: "All anybody seems to care about here is how they're dressed. This isn't religion; it's a fashion parade. Why does everyone only care how they look?"

Of course organized religion itches. It is trying to hold a crease in life. But what most adolescents fail to understand is the religious power of simply being seen and looking good in the "Big Room." It is a way of appearing before God, who we suspect is not beneath looking through the eyes of the community. Being seen by the congregation is like being seen by God. All those souls, together in that sanctuary, make something religious happen.

5

Acting like
the World Depends on It

PAGAN RELIGION INHABITS A UNIVERSE in which everything happens within circles of return. From days to months to years, from dreams to events to lifetimes, sooner or later, everything happens again and again forever. The task of religion in such a system is therefore to rehearse and celebrate those cycles—surely a noble and even sacred task. But there is more.

Judaism, especially as taught by the Hebrew prophets, brings to this world-view of cycles the linearity and non-repeatability of history. Some things, some very important things, just happen once. You only get one shot at them. For this reason, serious religion also necessitates politics. Yes, meditation in the prayer hall is vital, but equally so is taking to the streets. We are obligated, even commanded, to take responsibility for what is set before us, to step forward into our destiny, to try as best as we can to influence the way others behave and the way things happen. If we don't, someone else will.

Each day sets before us unique, unprecedented opportunities and challenges. More than a few of these have our names engraved on them. Most of the time, we are too busy or too conveniently self-deluded into thinking that our decision will have no consequence. Yet every now and then (from where does that thrilling and terrifying insight come upon us?), we feel compelled to act. Each one of us are messengers on a sacred mission. The world depends on it!

The Letter Tsadi

TSADI IS THE FIRST LETTER IN TIME. While other letters are first in the *aleph-beit* or in grace or even in importance, the first letter the Holy One formed was *tsadi*. For *tsadi* is righteousness, and "deeds of giving are the very foundation of the world." *Tsedek*, righteousness.

To make room for the other letters, the Lord of Hosts had to step back and remove *Godself*— in the way a father must restrain himself so that his little child will have room to grow. This is *tsimtsum*, self-withdrawal. Making yourself small so that another can grow.

Even so that you too can grow. Deeds of giving: deeds of making yourself less: deeds of making another more: such deeds are *tsadaka*. And one who does them, a righteous one, is a *tsaddik*. "The righteous shall inherit the earth."

No one can be a *tsaddik* alone. There must be at least nine others. We are able to rise to the rung of *tsadaka* only by binding ourselves with others who also could never make it alone. This then is a congregation, *tsibur*. *Tsadaka*, deeds of giving, are the reason for a congregation.

And this then is the reason that *tsadi* is the very foundation of the earth. The rock, *tsur*. The goal, *tsiyon*. And the mysterious fringes, *tsitsit*, which ever remind us of the commandments, our rock and our goal. "Make for yourselves fringes on the corners of your garments."

Politics of Repair

ENERGY IN THE FORM OF LIGHT IS TRAPPED in gross matter. Sparks of holiness are imprisoned in the stuff of creation. They yearn to be set free, reunited with their Source through human action. When we return something to its proper place, where it belongs, where it was meant to be; when we use something in a sacred way or for a holy purpose; when we treat another human being as a human being, the captive sparks are released and the cosmos is healed. This liberation of light is called the Repair of Creation.

The process occurs also within each individual. According to one legend, once there was a primordial person as big as the whole universe whose soul contained all souls. This macro-anthropos was the highest form of the Creator's self-manifestation. Light beamed through the human's eyes, nose, and mouth.

This person is identical with the universe and, for this reason, each human being is at the same time both riddled with divine sparks and in desperate need of repair. Each person is the whole world. And every human action therefore plays a role in the final restitution. Whatever we do is related to this ultimate task: to return all things to their original place in God. Everything a person does affects the process.

Repairing the World

IN SIXTEENTH-CENTURY SAFED, Rabbi Isaac Luria observed that in his world, like ours, many things seemed to be wrong. People suffered from hunger, disease, hatred, and war. "How could God allow such terrible things to happen?" wondered Luria. "Perhaps," he suggested, "it is because God needs our help." He explained his answer with a mystical story.

When first setting out to make the world, God planned to pour a Holy Light into everything in order to make it real. God prepared vessels to contain the Holy Light. But something went wrong. The light was so bright that the vessels burst, shattering into millions of broken pieces like dishes dropped on the floor. The Hebrew phrase that Luria used for this "breaking of the vessels" is *sh'virat ha-kaylim*.

Our world is a mess because it is filled with broken fragments. When people fight and hurt one another, they allow the world to remain shattered. The same can be said of people who have pantries filled with food and let others starve. According to Luria, we live in a cosmic heap of broken pieces, and God cannot repair it alone.

That is why God created us and gave us freedom of choice. We are free to do whatever we please with our world. We can allow things to remain broken or, as Luria urged, we can try to repair the mess. Luria's Hebrew phrase for "repairing the world" is *tikkun olam*.

As Jews, our most important task in life is to find what is broken in our world and repair it. The commandments in the Torah instruct us, not only on how to live as Jews, but on how to mend creation.

At the very beginning of the Book of Genesis (2:15), we read that God put Adam and Eve in the Garden of Eden and told them not to eat from the tree of knowledge. God also told them that it was their job to take care of the garden and to protect it.

The stories in the Torah tell not only of what happened long ago, but also of what happens in each generation. The stories happen over and over again in the life of each person. The Garden of Eden is our world, and we are Adam and Eve. When God says, "Take care of the garden and protect it," God is also saying, "Take care of your world and protect it."

According to one midrash, God showed Adam and Eve the Garden of Eden and said, "I have made the whole thing for you, so please take good care of it. If you wreck it, there will be no one else to repair it other than you." (*Kohelet Rabba* 7.13)

When you see something that is broken, fix it. When you find something that is lost, return it. When you see something that needs to be done, do it. In that way, you will take care of your world and repair creation. If all the people in the world were to do so, our world would truly be a Garden of Eden, the way God meant it to be. If everything broken could be repaired, then everyone and everything would fit together like the pieces of one gigantic jigsaw puzzle. But, for people to begin the great task of repairing creation, they first must take responsibility.

Messengers of the Most High

THE HEBREW WORD FOR ANGEL IS *MALACH*. Which also means messenger: one who is sent.

It does not mean cherubic creatures who adorn architecture, valentines, and fantasy. An angel can be anyone who is sent. Just as anyone who is sent can be an angel. It is required only that there be an errand. One message. As the midrash says, "One angel never performs two missions just as two angels never go on one mission." (*Bereshit Rabba* 50:2)

There is one great difference between people chosen to be God's messengers and earthly messengers. While those on errands of this world almost always know that they are sent and where and why, people chosen to be messengers of the Most High rarely even know that they are God's messengers. Unsuspecting and unaware. Consumed by their own plans and itineraries. Busy at work on their own schemes. God is already sending them somewhere else.

I do not know how many times in one's life one is a messenger. But for everyone it is at least once. One to whom it is given to know that his or her errand is completed is blessed and rare. Not so for most of us.

Remember only that you are not always going where you are going for the reasons you think you are.

There must have been a time when you entered a room and met someone and after a while you understood that unknown to either of you there was a reason you had met. You had changed the other or he or she had changed you. By some word or deed or just created by your presence, the errand had been completed. Then perhaps you were a little bewildered or humbled and grateful. And then it was over.

Each lifetime is the pieces of a jigsaw puzzle.
For some there are more pieces.
For others the puzzle is more difficult to assemble.
Some seem to be born with a nearly completed puzzle.
And so it goes.
Souls going this way and that
Trying to assemble the myriad parts.

But know this. You do not have within yourself
All the pieces to your puzzle.
Like before the days when they used to seal
jigsaw puzzles in cellophane. Insuring that
All the pieces were there.

Everyone carries with them at least one and probably
Many pieces to someone else's puzzle.
Sometimes they know it.
Sometimes they don't.

And when you present your piece
Which is worthless to you,
To another, whether you know it or not,
Whether they know it or not,
You are a messenger from the Most High.

We read in Genesis (18:1–2) that "the Lord appeared [to Abraham] by the terebinths of Mamre; He was sitting at the entrance of the tent at the heat of the day. Looking up, he saw three men [messengers] standing near him…"

Benno Jacob, the German Bible scholar, commenting on Abraham's intimacy with the Holy One, observes that "God appears to [Abraham] through three men; the closer a person's relationship to God, the more human is the form of God's manifestation."

The Zohar (I, 101a) is even more explicit: "And indeed whenever the celestial spirits descend to earth, they clothe themselves in physical things and appear to men in human shape."

ANOTHER ONE'S TEFILLIN

Tefillin are small black leather boxes containing bits of parchment on which are written prescribed paragraphs from the Torah. With leather straps they are bound—"for a sign upon thy hand and for frontlets between thine eyes" (Deuteronomy 6:8)—upon the forehead and the arm each morning. It is an act of personal devotion and obedience to the Master. Now these days *tefillin* are only regularly worn by observant traditional Jews. The rest of us wear them with less frequency, in between which times we store these sacred utensils in the back of the drawer where we also keep our socks.

I happen to have an idiosyncrasy when it comes to *tefillin*. Whenever I travel overnight, I carry my *tefillin* with me. I tell myself that just in case the spirit should move me, or if I should feel spiritually weakened, I would have them with me. Well, what can I say, after maybe several dozen trips I still haven't put them on but a few times. Nevertheless I still carry them. I even suggested once that I had stumbled upon some new commandment. The commandment of carrying your *tefillin* with you to hotel rooms.

Then, the other day, a dear friend told me that his mother had given away his set of *tefillin*. There were tears in his eyes when he told me.

And then I understood why I had carried my "unused" *tefillin* with me all this time. They weren't mine. I was only bringing them to their intended owner. "They must be yours," I said.

One of the most important people in the Torah remains nameless. His name, if indeed he has one, is subservient to the task he was sent to perform. He is known only by his deed. Sent by the Most High from another world to alter the course of this one. He is literally *deus ex machina*, a divine one, whose presence in the plot is awkwardly contrived. Some uninvited guest whose only function is to do one thing. And then, never to be heard from again. Perhaps he had an elaborate and full life. A constellation of intricate and interlocking relationships.

But so far as the Holy One is concerned he had but one moment. One task. Pressed into His service, who knows, perhaps against his will or even without his knowledge. A messenger who does not know he is a messenger. An actor with a one-line walk-on part. Unnamed in the program.

The Torah only calls him *ish*, "someone." Yet without him the children of Israel would never have stayed in Egypt. Never been freed. Never crossed the sea. Indeed, never come into being as a people.

In the final chapters of Genesis, we read in the Joseph saga of a favored and spoiled son. A boy whose bragging and dreams earn him the wrath of his brothers, who sold him to a caravan bound for Egypt and what they hoped would be oblivion. A boy whose gift as a dream interpreter set him second only to Pharaoh himself. A boy who acquired such power that he was able to manipulate his eleven brothers and father into coming down to Egypt and ultimately settling there. Clearly, the Torah means to teach us that it is all the doing of the Holy One. Event after event has the unmistakable mark of divine contrivance. But of all the scenes chronicling our descent into Egypt, none seems more superfluous and dramatically unnecessary than the scene in Shechem.

Joseph's father sent him to find out how things are going with his brothers whom they both believe are tending the flocks in

Shechem. But when he arrives there, they have already left. And we read:

"...And a man came upon him wandering in the fields. The man asked him, "What are you looking for?" He answered, "I am looking for my brothers. Could you tell me where they are pasturing!" The man said, "They have gone from here, for I heard them say: Let us go to Dothan." (Genesis 37:15–17)

Rabbi Moses ben Maimon teaches that "the 'man' was a messenger. And that this odd scene has not been for nothing."

Indeed were it not for the man who "happened" to find Joseph wandering in the fields, he would have returned home. Never been sold into slavery. Never brought his family down to Egypt. The Jewish people would have never become slaves. And there could have been no Jewish people at all.

We are all only *ish*, someone. No more and no less than the unnamed stranger of the empty pastures of Shechem, without whose one line, "I heard them say, 'let us go to Dothan...'" the Holy One's intention could not be realized.

And so we understand that ordinary people are messengers of the Most High. They go about their tasks in holy anonymity. Often, even unknown to themselves. Yet, if they had not been there, if they had not said what they said or did what they did, it would not be the way it is now. We would not be the way we are now. Never forget that you, too, may be a messenger. Perhaps even one whose errand extends over several lifetimes.

Reconsidering Rabbinic Power

In Hasidism, each soul has a central life teaching, as it were, a "torah." For the *gedolim,* or "great ones of the generation," their teaching is so bright that it refracts itself in a myriad of ways. This is certainly true about my teacher, Arnold Jacob Wolf, and his extraordinary example of how rabbis can serve their congregations. After a quarter century as a rabbi, I am still amazed by his insight. But before I try to identify Wolf's "torah," let me begin with three of its implications.

As a spiritual self-discipline, the rabbi must always tell the truth to his congregation, not only in private, but also, and especially, in public, no matter how embarrassing, frightening, or funny it sounds. The rabbi should speak this truth in ordinary and, if necessary, even blunt language. He should call things for what they are and as he sees them. He should not curry favor with the prominent or the wealthy, nor with the modest or the weak. This means: no obsequiousness, no politicking, no glad handing, and no baby kissing. Ultimately, I suspect, this also means very little formal job security.

Since religious institutions are by nature uniquely prone to self-delusion (they are, after all, the custodians of divine truth and righteousness on earth!), who if not the rabbi should say, "Cut the Mickey Mouse!" or "We should be ashamed of ourselves"! He must not be afraid to speak to lay people about their congregation in the same language they speak about their own businesses or professional practices. By exempting religious institutions from the sharp candor of everyday language, we deprive them of their best chance for vitality.

The rabbi must not take himself or his congregation too seriously. Wolf would say, "We are the wise men of Chelm [legendary dummies]!" Indeed, the rabbi must go out of his way to laugh at his own foibles and the congregation's sacred cows. Wolf once taught, "Religion is a serious business, but this congregation is a joke." On another occasion, he said, "Just whom do we think we're fooling? It couldn't be God."

In an age when so many rabbis confused their titles with their first names, wore black robes, had reserved parking spaces, and portraits of themselves festooning the foyers, my teacher, Rabbi Arnold Wolf, was called "Arnold" by his congregants, had no secretary, and routinely confessed his mistakes from the pulpit. Most of his congregants were convinced this was a clever, Machiavellian manipulation, but it was only the truth. Wolf taught that jokes and unpretentiousness remind everyone that we are just ordinary human beings, especially the rabbi.

By demystifying the rabbi-congregation relationship, Wolf sought to liberate it from transference and fantasy. He counseled rabbis to think of the congregation as the place where they worked and, like any other employee anywhere, to ask about the working conditions, the hours, the salary, and the time off. "I only work here," Wolf would quip. "Come to think of it, if I didn't work here, I'd probably *daven* at a little Orthodox place downtown." As an employee, he should neither have to pay dues nor be entitled to vote. The rabbi should routinely absent himself from board of directors meetings and the congregation's annual meeting to give all of his "bosses" a forum to evaluate his performance on the job.

Wolf was fond of reminding me that rabbis did not own their congregations nor should they try to manage or run them. Lay people must run their congregations because they are the ones who pay for them. Lay people must be genuinely free to do whatever they like with their congregation, including, Wolf once said, electing an anti-Semite to be president. He once went so far as to say that how a congregation gets and spends its money is none of the rabbi's business. The rabbi's job is to teach the Jews whatever he knows about how to grow in the service of the Holy One and then get out of the way while they figure out for themselves how to make the thing work.

This brings us closer to the core of what I believe is Wolf's unique conception, or torah, of the rabbi-congregation relationship. Surely no one has said it with greater clarity or force. Indeed many dismiss it as just charisma or insist that it is impossible. But there are some who understand that it may be the key to revitalizing the American synagogue.

Wolf's torah of congregational life teaches that the rabbi does not own the congregation. Its members own it. They pay for it and they must be the ones who get to decide what to do with it. The rabbi must be ever vigilant not to let the congregation become an extension of his ego. Precisely because it is not his but theirs, congregants will be able to do what they want with their congregation without fear of the rabbi taking it personally. Wolf once cautioned me never to speak of it as "my" congregation but rather, "the congregation where I work. You are only its guide and teacher, devoted to helping Jews understand the implications of using their own power." The rabbi should have no contract; as Wolf often joked, "My bags are always packed."

Paradoxically, renouncing rabbinic power may be the rabbi's best shot at attaining occupational security! (One of my colleagues calls this "rabbinic judo.") Whenever a rabbi gets into a power struggle, even if he wins, he loses. The only exceptions, Wolf once counseled, are matters involving potential personal injury. Then the rabbi must use everything at his disposal to ensure that folks behave with decency toward one another.

Such an attitude of rabbinic powerlessness guarantees communal vitality. If the rabbi "runs" nothing and is only free to speak his mind, then everything is literally "in play." Lay leaders will be neither puppets nor personal opponents. And after a while, those gifted with real competence and creativity will rise to leadership. Discussion will revolve less around the person of the rabbi and more around his teaching. And in this way the members of the congregation will be able to get on with the sacred business of helping one another and serving the Holy One.

ORIGINALLY PUBLISHED IN *MANNA* MAGAZINE
(GREAT BRITAIN), 1996

Two Jewish Mothers

A FEW YEARS AGO I WAS INVITED to offer a few lectures in the United Kingdom. Being an Anglophile, I was delighted by the opportunity. But there were complications—committees, calendars, administrative matters, and things didn't work out. I was disappointed, but didn't think much more about it until over a year later, a friend in England casually mentioned about how unfortunate it was that I was "purged" from teaching.

"What do you mean?" I asked.

"Well, you know," he said, trying to be discreet, "when they heard about how you had officiated at a 'commitment ceremony' between two lesbians, you became too hot for all the Orthodox and even a few of the liberals to handle. Even though many of us have been fighting the good fight, apparently some thought it was better to just cut you loose."

It is true. I did officiate at a ceremony uniting two lesbians. They were both Jewish. They met at our synagogue. One even "came out" at a *Shabbat* morning Torah discussion. They had bought a house in town so they could be close to their congregation. So, when they came to me, their rabbi, and asked if I would help them consecrate their new Jewish home with some kind of "wedding-like" ceremony, I had to take their request very seriously. I shared my intention with the board of directors of the congregation, who (in one of their finest hours, God bless them all) voted to support my decision, unanimously.

The process of making my decision was lengthy, serious, and spiritual: It was nothing less than the intersection of spirituality and politics and a way to keep us all talking out in the open about spiritual reality.

I had a cousin who moved to California as soon as he was discharged from the army. He had some kind of job in the arts out there, working for network television or something. I only met him on a few occasions when the entire family gathered in Detroit for a major event. He was, as I recall, a very kind, gentle man, with a warm, perceptive smile and a good sense of humor. And while it seemed odd that he chose to live so far away from an otherwise very close family, I never paid it much attention. He died a few years ago. Some members of the family said he died of pneumonia. And we all know what that means. It means they thought he died of AIDS. And that means he was gay. And that means that there was something ontologically wrong with him and that his voluntary excommunication and disease were an appropriate punishment.

That's how the last generation dealt with homosexuals. We sent them into *cherem*, into exile. They were sick. Perverse. They corrupted children. They compulsively hung around restrooms and sodomized little boys. They were an abomination. Some people thought the reason men were gay was because they had overbearing mothers and weak fathers. Others thought that homosexuality was just moral weakness. Maybe it was partly genetic. We created an elaborate infrastructure of half-truths to justify our actions and even make us feel righteous. If the twentieth century has taught us anything, it is that people, without hesitation, will humiliate, wound, even butcher a person whom society has identified is not like them. It is almost as if people seem to have a need to exclude others in order to make themselves feel secure. We Jews know all about that.

To makes matters worse, virtually everyone has some cause to feel insecure in his or her sexual identity. And someone who is homosexual threatens our own, often tenuous, self-definitions.

According to Kinsey, sexual orientation fluctuates over a lifetime. Fifty per cent of the male population is exclusively heterosexual throughout adulthood; four per cent is exclusively homosexual; and forty-six per cent have both heterosexual and homosexual inclinations in the course of their adult lives. Among women, the incidence of homosexuality is from one-third to one-half less than among men. And, as psychotherapy has conclusively demonstrated, regardless of actual behavior, everyone has latent homosexual fantasies.

What would it be like to live as a homosexual in our society? Your family would treat you funny. They might buy you a ticket to some faraway place. Your sex urge would be defined as immoral, perverse, pathological. You would be subject to de facto job discrimination. If you had a lifelong, homosexual partner, with whom you had lived in fidelity and love for forty years, none of the legal benefits of taxation or inheritance would apply. If you were critically ill, your partner would not have the hospital visitation rights automatically accorded a spouse. If you were a Jew and did not want to flaunt who you were but did not want to hide it either, there would be very few places you could *daven*.

A cursory reading of the traditional sources (such as Leviticus 18) seems to equate incest, sexual perversion, and homosexuality. But this is an egregious error. God's Torah is not just a law; it is a way of love and compassion. To be sure, the Torah's moral principles remain constant from generation to generation, but as our knowledge of what happens in the secret places of the home, the bedroom, and the psyche increases, we are better able to understand and apply them.

SEVEN MYTHS ABOUT GAYS

We live in an extraordinary time in the evolution of Jewish moral awareness, and as liberal Jews, we are on its cutting edge. It was only recently that pregnant women were allowed to appear in public. And only a generation ago, even Jewish husbands were allowed to discreetly abuse their wives and children, and many did. It is not a sign of moral weakness or decay to speak of such painful parts of our history. On the contrary, doing so is a sign of moral courage and vitality.

And so, as serious liberal Jews who believe that our tradition constantly demands we sensitize ourselves to social reality, we must fashion a new framework for conceiving of homosexuality. Rabbi Bradley Shavit Artson, writing in *Tikkun* magazine, outlines the classic arguments against homosexuality.[1] They are all specious and insidious.

Argument #1: Homosexuality is unnatural. Biologists have conclusively demonstrated that homosexuality among mammals is not unusual. And one study of seventy-six different cultures found that in sixty-four per cent some sort of homosexual behavior was accepted for certain members of the community.

Argument #2: Homosexuality is a mental illness. According to the unanimous vote of the American Psychiatric Association in 1973, "homosexual acts are not by themselves psychiatric disorders." Period. Even Freud acknowledged that "homosexuality… is nothing to be ashamed of… it cannot be classified as an illness." Psychologist Sol Gordon has pointed out that a child's sexual orientation is determined by the time he or she is five years old, and Nathaniel Lehrman writes that "homosexuals rarely become heterosexuals even with the best treatment methods supposedly available." To say it directly, there is no cure because there is no illness.

Argument #3: Homosexuality is disgusting. This argument is at least candid. But perhaps you can remember back to a time when imagining any sexual act was disgusting. Indeed, most of us would probably find many acts that routinely occur within healthy heterosexual families also disgusting. But in those cases, however, social sanctions are never invoked. Somehow only physical expressions of homosexual love are intolerable. To describe a mutually loving and respectful intimacy as disgusting only betrays our ignorance and usually a deeper personal fear of our own latent homosexuality. It certainly describes nothing intrinsic to homosexual love.

Argument #4: Homosexuals are bad ego models for young people. In its ugliest formulation, this argument maintains that socially sanctioned homosexuals serve not only as dangerous role models for young children, but by insinuation, that homosexuals will impose their perverse will on children. Even granting the highly theoretical and extremely unlikely existence of a person with no sexual preference, how will we explain the existence of all the homosexuals who managed to discover who they were with absolutely no role models at all? Despite overwhelming evidence that the preponderance of sexual assaults on children are committed by heterosexual men, homophobia prevails. What must be said instead, loudly and clearly, is that people who abuse children, whether heterosexual or homosexual, are pathological and their actions are criminal.

Argument #5: Publicly sanctioned homosexuality will increase the number of homosexuals. This is perhaps the most intriguing argument. According to this line of reasoning, since most men and women at some time in their sexual development could "go either way," social tolerance of homosexual behavior might make a few more people homosexuals who might otherwise be nudged into being heterosexual. But the scientific research of the past few decades conclusively demonstrates that this is simply inaccurate. We now know that regardless of opposition or tolerance, some people in every age turn out to be gay, and the greatest difference between periods is not in the proportion of the population that is gay, but in the way sexual preference is expressed. We also know that children raised in gay or lesbian households grow up to be heterosexual at precisely the same rates as children raised in heterosexual homes. Let us suppose, for the purposes of argument, that publicly sanctioned homosexuality would actually increase the number of homosexuals, and that this would be deleterious to society. How then shall we responsibly go about discouraging homosexuality? What social penalties shall we condone? How many homosexuals must be psychologically damaged in order to stigmatize their conduct? And at what point is this alleged good to society by discouraging homosexual behavior offset by the abuse done to completely innocent human beings who happen to be homosexuals? Dr. Eugene Borowitz, Reform Judaism's preeminent ethicist, correctly points out that simply fearing that tolerating homosexuality might encourage people of uncertain sexuality and those whose psyches or traumas make acting-out attractive to abandon heterosexuality cannot morally justify denying homosexuals equal rights.

Argument #6: Homosexuality destroys family life. At a time when marriages often occurred between teenagers, the discovery by one of the partners that he or she was a homosexual probably was a common home wrecker. But what ruins family life even more is dehumanizing and exiling our own children and trying to compel them to lead celibate lives while denying them equal social and religious status.

Argument #7: Homosexuality is explicitly and unequivocally forbidden by the Torah, which calls it an abomination. "If a man lies with a male as one lies with a woman, the two of them have done an abhorrent thing. They shall be put to death." (Leviticus 20:13) "No Israelite woman shall be a cult prostitute, nor shall any Israelite man be a cult prostitute." (Deuteronomy 23:18) "Do not lie with a male as one lies with a woman; it is an abhorrence." (Leviticus 18:22) Scholarship reveals a different situation. Cultic prostitution was widespread throughout the ancient Near East, with both genders servicing male worshippers. Twice the Hebrew Bible tells of Jewish kings who expelled male prostitutes from the temple. In both instances the prostitutes were linked explicitly with idol worship. The Levitical prohibitions refer to rites of idolatrous prostitution and the transgressions of Sodom and Gomorrah to a violation of the ancient Near Eastern code of hospitality. Even more significant, Artson observes that there is not a single case in the Hebrew Bible or in any rabbinic legal literature until the middle of the twentieth century that deals with homosexual acts in the context of homosexual love. Every biblical case deals with heterosexuals who engage in homosexual acts. In other words, when Jewish religious tradition speaks of a "homosexual" it bears little resemblance to the way we now understand such a person.

Opening Our Hearts to Who We Are

What we do know about homosexuality is that we don't know what makes someone homosexual. Anyone's child could turn out to be homosexual. Whatever it is that makes a man or a woman homosexual, according to the best available scientific knowledge, seems to have virtually nothing to do with parents, society, or mental health.

In every culture the number of homosexuals seems to remain constant. Statistics suggest the number is somewhere between five and ten per cent of the general population. So no matter what we do or don't do, a finite number of human beings will be gay or lesbian.

People we know and love will be—or already are—homosexuals. Many of them are our own children. And there is absolutely nothing we can or should do to try to change that. Homosexuality is an unalterable aspect of personality.

We cannot ask homosexuals to practice celibacy. Love and its expression in all forms of human activity, including sexuality, are an indispensable dimension of human fulfillment. Indeed, in our refusal to legitimate monogamous homosexual relationships, we discourage them from establishing stable families.

While the present social reality makes the creation of "gay" congregations unavoidable, we should try to fashion a Jewish community in which everyone is welcome and respected without regard to his or her sexual preference.

There is no moral or religious reason why two men or two women cannot establish monogamous, nurturing, loving relationships and families. Homosexual couples are perfectly able to raise healthy children. Indeed given the child-rearing disasters we have all witnessed within heterosexual families, it is difficult to imagine how homosexual parents could make things any worse.

We are all obligated to help every human being realize his or her fullest God-given potential in what ever body, psyche, and soul they were issued. As Professor Ellen Umansky has scolded: Who are we to declare that the way in God has created certain people is an abomination? And who are we to deny other human beings the joys of companionship on the grounds that their needs are not identical to our own? Our goal must be nothing short of full acceptance. As Rabbi Joel Kahn said, "God does not create in vain."

Someone asked me how it felt to stand beneath a *chuppa* with two women. I could not take offense at the question, for I had been curious myself. But the answer came as a surprise. It felt like standing under any *chuppa* with two people who are in love and about to consecrate a Jewish home. They looked radiant, joyous, in love. Out of the corner of my eye, I even caught sight of one bride's mother. She was beaming with pride, just like any other mother whose child had found a life partner and a congregation to call home.

There are a few interesting aftershocks to all this. One family that quit the congregation in protest, they subsequently rejoined. Three other lesbian couples have joined and are indistinguishable from any other household. One of the couples, through artificial insemination, gave birth to a child, whom they named in the synagogue. I held the baby in front of the ark and saw her parents in front of me. I said the standard ritual, including the part about "Torah, good deeds, and *chuppa*," then I couldn't resist suggesting that there could be no doubt about the Jewishness of this little girl who, after all, had not one, but two Jewish mothers.

Stranger on the Bus

A LIGHT SNOW WAS FALLING and the streets were crowded with people. It was Munich in Nazi Germany. One of my rabbinic students, Shifra Penzias, told me her great-aunt, Sussie, had been riding a city bus home from work when SS storm troopers suddenly stopped the coach and began examining the identification papers of the passengers. Most were annoyed, but a few were terrified. Jews were being told to leave the bus and get into a truck around the corner.

My student's great-aunt watched from her seat in the rear as the soldiers systematically worked their way down the aisle. She began to tremble, tears streaming down her face. When the man next to her noticed that she was crying, he politely asked her why.

"I don't have the papers you have. I am a Jew. They're going to take me."

The man exploded with disgust. He began to curse and scream at her. "You stupid bitch," he roared. "I can't stand being near you!"

The SS men asked what all the yelling was about.

"Damn her," the man shouted angrily. "My wife has forgotten her papers again! I'm so fed up. She always does this!"

The soldiers laughed and moved on.

My student said that her great-aunt never saw the man again. She never even knew his name.

YOU ARE GOING ABOUT YOUR BUSINESS when you stumble onto something that has your name on it. Or, to be more accurate, a task with your name on it finds you. Its execution requires inconvenience, self-sacrifice, even risk. You step forward and encounter your destiny. This does not mean you must do everything that lands on your doorstep, or that you should assume every risk or make every self-sacrifice. But it does mean that you must tell yourself the truth about where you have been placed and why.

You do not exercise your freedom by doing what you want. Self-indulgence is not an exercise of freedom. But when you accept the task that destiny seems to have set before you, you become free. Perhaps the only exercise of real freedom comes from doing what you were meant to do all along.

If everything is connected to everything else, then everyone is ultimately responsible for everything. We can blame *nothing* on anyone else. The more we comprehend our mutual interdependence, the more we fathom the implications of our most trivial acts. We find ourselves within a luminous organism of sacred responsibility.

Even on a bus in Munich.

ORIGINALLY PUBLISHED IN *THE JEWISH REPORTER*,
FRAMINGHAM, MASSACHUSETTS, 1994

Rewriting the Past

TOM WOLFE'S NOVEL *THE RIGHT STUFF*, chronicles the beginnings of America's manned space flight program. One of the early scenes in the movie version takes place up in the Mojave desert at a tavern where those early test pilots hung out after the day's work. The bartender was a crusty old coot who served up drinks and sage quips to the men who had the right stuff. One of those pilots was the young Chuck Yaeger, played by Sam Shephard, a handsome swashbuckling, horse-riding pilot, chasing the gremlins who lived beyond the sound barrier. The man cast to play the bartender and counsel the young Chuck Yaeger is the real-life Chuck Yaeger. Is there anything you would like to tell the person who is playing who you were several decades ago?

Over time, things change meaning. I am reminded of how one of my children took a rare book I loved and innocently used a few pages of it for a coloring book. At the time, I was furious. But now, as I reflect on those scribblings, they bring not only nostalgia but tenderness. What was once a source of anger, is now a source of great love.

Abraham Isaac Kook, the first chief Ashkenazi rabbi of Jerusalem, observed that "what [we] desire is tied up with what [we have] done...Since nothing is totally eradicated the will can impose a special configuration on past actions...[But] once the will has put on it a configuration of the good, it itself becomes a stimulant for good and delight, the joy in God and [God's] light."

In this way, the present can change the past. *Teshuva*, the act of returning to whom you *meant* to be, can change who we were. It cannot change what we did, but it can change the meaning of what we did. In so doing, it can change the future. Don't make *teshuva* because it will make some pain go away. Make *teshuva* because it will send you back to who you were, change it into who you meant to be, and in so doing change you into whom you might still become.

Obviously, we cannot undo the past. What is done is done. But what we do now about what we did then, while not altering the past deed itself, can place it into a new context of meaning. By our present actions, we can effectively reach back through the otherwise impermeable membrane that seals the past and thus reshape it. For example, we may have injured someone with a thoughtless remark long ago. Now we not only acknowledge, regret, and repudiate what we did, we devote ourselves to repairing the damage. We not only make amends and through them make ourselves into a finer person, we also heal the pain so that now in the light of our present turning, both the one we injured and ourselves regard our original transgression as the initiation of this greater intimacy and love. We have placed the initial damage into a larger constellation of meaning. Isolated, the past evil deed is only a great shame. But seen from the present, as the commencement of this new turning, the meaning of the original deed has been transformed and the past is rewritten.

Rabbi Yehuda Aryeh Leib of Ger, in the *Sefas Emes,* takes this idea even farther. He begins with Joseph's consolation to his brothers. "And now, do not be sad or reproach yourselves because you sold me down here; for it was to save life that God sent me ahead of you." (Genesis 45:5) Indeed, every cause issues from the Source of All Causes.

When the one who sins makes *teshuva* from love every sin is actually transformed into a merit. As our verse reads, "So now it was not you who sent me here but God." (Genesis 45:8) This is just the way things were meant to be from the very beginning. They sold me into slavery. But now, the *teshuva* has transformed [and revealed] everything to be just the way God intended it. And all because you made *teshuva* in love. So whatever you do, don't be sad.

In other words, through the act of *teshuva*, we can literally transform past sins into present merits. Perhaps this is why we are advised to make *teshuva* on Yom Kippur, as well as on every Sabbath eve, because through it, we are able to heal and perfect the past week and join God in saying, "Behold it is good."

A God Who
Looks like Nothing

I was reading the mail in my office at the synagogue when one of our fourth grade teachers came running in.

"Rabbi, we need you right away: The children are talking about God!"

I went down to the classroom and began my emergency lesson. "Tell me what you know about God," I asked them. A few hands slowly went up.

"God made the world," said one.

I wrote, "Made the world," on the board.

"God's one." Said another. I put it on the board too.

"God's good," ventured a third. There were a few dissenting votes, but the majority was still for divine beneficence.

Then another child said, "God's invisible." I started to write it on the board, but another student objected.

"You're wrong. God's visible. He's [*sic*] right here, right now."

"Oh yeah, I don't see Him. What's He look like?"

To which the other said (and I'm not making this up), "That's just it…there's nothing to see!"

So that's it, I was instructed by the nine-year-old, it's not that you shouldn't make any graven images of God. You can't! Not only is God's name made of vowel letters and therefore effectively the sound of breathing, and not only is the only thing God says at Sinai the letter *aleph*, which is only the noise you make as you begin to make any sound. But God doesn't look like anything at all.

You simply can't sell this sort of stuff in shopping malls and airports:

"What's this God's name?"

"The sound of breathing."

"What's this God say?"

"Only the softest, barely audible noise."

"And what's this God look like?"

"Nothing!"

(This might also explain why there are so few Jews in the world.)

The theological and psychological implications of all this should not be underestimated. The goal is serving God, to get your self out of the way, to make your self as nothing in service of the One who looks like nothing. Paradoxically, you must lose your self in order to find it. Perhaps this is also what the Kabbalists had in mind when they named God the *Ayn Sof*, the One of Nothing.

The Letter Hay

HAY HAS ALMOST A SOUND. The sound of breathing out. The most effortless noise a soul can make. And that is why there is some of *hay* in every word. And also why *hay* is so elusive, for it is the sound of being present, *hay*. The letter drawn by two marks facing one another.

Hay is the closest you can come to the Holy One. God says to each of us, "*Ehyeh asher ehyeh*, I will be who I will be." *Hay*. Hey! I will be who I will be. Not who you want Me to be!

When two people are married, they look at each other and whisper: *Hay*, "*Haray aht miku-deshet li*, Behold, I will try with all my being to be present for you." And so the *hay* of *hoo*, which means "he," and the *hay* of *hee*, which means "she," become the *hay* of *haym*, which means "them."

But there is still a greater *hay* than "behold." And this is the *hay* of "*heenayni*, Here I am."

While everyone can say, "I am present," only a very few can say "*Heenayni*, Here am I." For to answer *heenayni* means that you no longer belong only to yourself. To answer *heenayni* means that you give the *hay* of your being over to the One who calls. That is why *hay* is the letter most often linked with God's Name.

Breathing the Name of God

THE LETTERS OF THE NAME OF GOD in Hebrew are *yod, hay, vav,* and *hay.* They are frequently mispronounced as "*Yahveh.*" But in truth they are unutterable. Not because of the holiness they evoke, but because they are all vowels and you cannot pronounce all the vowels at once without risking respiratory injury.

This word is the sound of breathing. The holiest Name in the world, the Name of the Creator, is the sound of your own breathing.

That these letters are unpronounceable is no accident. Just as it is no accident that they are also the root letters of the Hebrew verb "to be." Scholars have suggested that a reasonable translation of the four-letter Name of God might be: The One Who Brings Into Being All That Is. So God's Name is the Name of Being itself. And, since God is holy, then so is all creation. At the burning bush, Moses asks God for God's Name, but God only replies with *Ehyeh-asher-ehyeh,* which is often incorrectly rendered by the static English, "I am who I am." But in truth the Hebrew future is unequivocal: "I will be who I will be." Here is a Name (and a God) who is neither completed nor finished. This God is literally not yet.

"I" Is the Lord Your God

WITH THE EXCEPTION OF ONE WORD, human words and Divine words cannot be the same. Infinite language cannot be mortal speech, except for one word—the first person singular pronoun "I," "*Anochi*." For just this is the name each self has for its self. And, since the gesture of self-reference—the way by which I evoke who I am—is the same for every self, whenever we say "I" we evoke not only the "I" of every other soul, we echo the primary "I," "*Anochi*," of Sinai. Whatever makes each individual unique, that innermost core self, is precisely what we each share with one another, and with our creator. We are made of the same holy stuff. It has this mysterious ability to look different in each pair of eyes, to sound different in each voice, but it is all the same.

PRAYING BY THE OCEAN

Professor Richard Rubenstein of Bridgeport University in Connecticut offers a classical and elegant explanation of this relationship we have with God: God is the ocean and we are the waves. In some sense, each wave has its moment in which it is distinguishable as a somewhat separate entity. Nevertheless, no wave is entirely distinct from the ocean.... The waves are surface manifestations of the ocean. Our knowledge of the ocean is largely dependent on the way it manifests itself in the waves.[1]

But you cannot simultaneously be aware that you are the wave and be aware that you are part of the ocean. And that is why God is so elusive. In a similar vein, theologian Alan Watts suggests that "God is the self of the world, but you can't see God for the same reason that, without a mirror, you can't see your own eyes...."[2] Consider, for instance, what such an idea would do to our understanding of prayer.

Assuming that the waves could speak, what should they say to the ocean? Perhaps the most meaningful noise they could make would be the rhythmic, relentless whisper they make as they rise and fall, as they come in and out of being. Surely that is a worthy prayer. Surely those prayerful sounds, if they could be scored on paper, would be worthy of regular rehearsal, for they would remind each wave of the source of its being. Making those sounds would remind each wave that it was indeed a wave and, contrary to all the wave's illusions, not something else.

You might say that we have only two options: We can recite the words, acknowledge that we are all waves of the same sea, made of the same stuff, creatures of the same Creator. Or we can be too busy to make the words, recite the prayer, offer the service.

We can, on occasion, to select another analogy, choose to be aware of the barely audible noise made by the involuntary emptying and filling of our lungs, this noise by which we live. Or, we can ignore it, take it for granted. The only casualty is our own awareness, our sense of life.

The prayers run in two directions, for the ocean also speaks to the waves. But since the waves are already part of the ocean, their sound is, in some sense, the sound of their source speaking to them. They are the mouth of the ocean, and their prayer is the way the sea has of speaking to itself.

In the same way, the words of the prayerbook and meditations of our hearts are the sound of God speaking to God. As Rabbi Kalnoymos Kalmish Shapira of Piesetzna, who perished in the Warsaw ghetto, used to say, "Not only does God hear our prayers, God prays them through us as well."

Other Hasidim went even further. They equated the one who prays with the very prayer that is offered: "You are your prayer." Until finally prayer, the one who offers it, and the One who hears it are one and the same. Theologians Arthur Green and Barry Holtz observe that:

> The worshiper continues to recite the words of prayer, but it is no longer the worshiper who speaks them. Rather it is the Presence who speaks through him. In that prayerful return to the source one has reached the highest human state, becoming nought but the passive instrument for the ever self-proclaiming praise of God.[3]

Imagine that the double helix coil of deoxyribonucleic acid in your genes wanted to speak to the double helix coil of deoxyribonucleic acid in your father and mother. Your parents' DNA would say, "Why do you speak to us? Does not everything you have and everything you are already come from us? Together, we are the source of your uniqueness."

So it is with us and God during prayer. What more is there to say except to acknowledge this primal mystery with ritualized regularity and religious ecstasy. Indeed, for this reason perhaps the only worthwhile conversation is to rehearse routinely that ancient truth, morning, afternoon, and evening. "Oh Lord, open my lips that my mouth may declare your praise." (Psalm 51:17)

LOSING YOUR SOUL TO THE FIRST WORD

If encountering God means loss of self, it is little wonder that our ancestors were so ambivalent at Sinai. If a person got too close, heard too much, he or she might never come back.

When the Israelites heard the word "*Anochi*," which was the "I" of the ten utterances at Mount Sinai, their souls left them. The Divine utterance returned to the Holy One, and said: "Sovereign of the Universe, You are full of life, and Your Torah is full of life. But You have sent me to the dead. They are all dead!" Thereupon God made sweetened the word for them [and made it less powerful].

Rabbi Simeon bar Yohai explained that the Torah, which the Holy One then gave to Israel, restored their souls to them. (*Shemot Rabba* 29:3) That is why it is said in Psalm 19:8, "The Torah of the Lord is perfect, restoring the soul." It brings us back to life.

EVERYTHING IN ONE WORD

Hebrew has no verb "to be" in the present tense. This means that there is no way to say "am," "is," or "are" and that any attempt to speak of "being," at least in the present, only can be inferred from context but never spoken. The language creates its own circumlocutions, and Hebrew speakers carry on ordinary lives in the present tense like everyone else. But in the case of the first of the ten utterances at Sinai, we are left with one tantalizing ambiguity.

Those seven Hebrew words translated into literal English are: "I Lord your-God who brought-you from- the-Land-of Egypt." So while they can mean, "I am the Lord, your God…" they can just as easily and properly be rendered, "I (*Anochi*) is the Lord your God."

Furthermore, according to the Midrash, the passage in Exodus, "And God spoke all these words, saying" (Exodus 20:1) means that "God spoke all the ten commandments with one utterance." (*Bamidbar Rabba* 11:7) Just think of it: Everything rolled within the seed of the first utterance (II *Zohar* 85b)—I (*Anochi*), the Name of God, and the source of our own selfhood.

I AM AND DO NOT COVET

As the first utterance begins with "I," so the last commandment concludes with "your neighbor," thereby completing the spectrum from me to you, from one to another, from I to Thou. By the time the echo of that first, almost soundless *aleph* has reached the last commandment, "Do not covet," it seems to have lost most of its power. Not only is wanting what other people have unenforceable, it is virtually universal. How trivial this prohibition against coveting when set next to The Name of the Self of the Universe. Nevertheless, ac-

cording to Rabbi Yakum, "One who violates the tenth commandment violates them all" (*Pesikta Rabbati* 21:17), even the first!

The first utterance and the last commandment may be joined
to one another because they are simply different sides of the same
truth. They are each the cause of the other. Something like this is
suggested by Rabbi Michal of Zolotchov, who intuits that "not to
covet" is not a commandment but a reward.

If you are content with your portion, you will want nothing
and you will lack nothing. You will be like the One who spoke "I
am." It does not mean that you will not—nor ought not—change
and grow; it means only that at this moment, in this place you are
all that you can be. No more, no less. You simply will be present in
this *makom*, place, and by so being resemble the One who is also
called *makom*, place. It is almost a tautology. Right now we can only
be who we are. We are simply all that we can be. And once we recognize this, we can no longer covet anything because at this moment
there is nothing else that we could possibly be. And if that is so,
when I say "I am" I come very close to the One who spoke the first "I
am." Through fulfilling the prohibition against coveting, we have at
the same time "heard" the first utterance in a new way. To utter the
"I am" is to want nothing else, and strange though it sounds, to
want nothing else is the necessary prerequisite for all genuine growth.
The last commandment then is another way of saying the first utterance, and together they are the touchstone for all spiritual growth.
Growth must begin with self-acceptance; change begins with not
trying to change.

What you imagine you must do in order to change yourself is often
the very force that keeps you precisely the way you are. How else
can you explain the years and decades of your own foiled plans for
growth and broken resolutions? Consumed by an apparent passion
to be "other" than who you are, you try to be who you are not, but
in so doing succeed only in being a person who is trying to be other

than who you are. Thus the goal of all therapy is self-discovery, not the discovery of another self but one's true self. Beneath all the layers of wanting to be different, self-dissatisfaction, pretense, charade, and denial is a self. This self is a living dynamic force within everyone. And if you could remain still long enough here, now, in this very place, you would discover who you are. And by discovering who you are, you would at last be free to discover who you yet also might be. Layers of pretense and self-delusion fall away, leaving the innermost essence that knows its origin and destiny. This is a self that knows its place among other selves, perhaps not "I am" but "i am." This "i" is the dynamic force behind personal change. Who are we? Really? Not the public personae, nor the images, nor the professions, nor the apologies. Not the past, for that can only produce pride or guilt. Not the future, for that can only produce hope or fear. The first utterance is in the present. All that is said is the personal pronoun in the first person singular form: "*Anochi*, I."

The prohibition against coveting produces the same effect. If we are forbidden even to want anything belonging to someone else, we are left with only what is already ours. Do not covet her spouse or her house or her servants. Do not wish for his talent or his status or his style. Do not envy his past or her future. Instead accept your own. Not with stoic resignation but with quiet dignity. At this moment (at least) things could be no other way. Only once you are able to know this will you again understand (hear) the "I am" that begins (and perhaps concludes) every revelation.

HEARING THE SELF OF SINAI

I'll tell you what happened to Moses on Sinai. There was nothing audible, except his own breathing. Nothing visible that a video camera would pick up. And nothing different, except a new and strangely powerful sense of who he was. Now, for the first time, he knew that he was a discrete and autonomous human being. He knew furthermore that this sense—which later generations would call a self—was

somehow mysteriously the result of and therefore eternally co\
nected to some greater Self.

So many years earlier as a young shepherd he had sensed this
but did not know what to call it. All he knew then, as he watched a
bush burn (for what seemed like an eternity), was that somehow he
himself also could be on fire and not be consumed. And now on top
of the same mountain, here it was again, the same sensation, only
this time clear and unmistakable.

Now the first person singular pronoun, "*Anochi*, I" meant something new and unimaginable. His sister had told him, when he was
a little boy, that it was simply called the *aleph* of creation, the first
letter that was the mother of all articulate speech.[4] But here hidden,
trembling behind the rocks, he understood that this *aleph* was also
the first letter not only for the Holy One of all Being, but also the
name by which every person addresses his or her own self: "I." *Aleph*,
the first letter of the Hebrew alphabet, and the letter that began
God's invisible speech at Sinai, is also the first letter of the Hebrew
word "*Anochi*, I."

For this reason, Sinai occurs whenever we re-experience that
first barely audible letter that begins the name of *Anochi*, "I," the
Self. Whenever, in other words, like Moses, we are quiet long enough
to become aware of the barely audible noise of our own breathing.

Project Sense of Self onto God

God is our sense of self, our innermost essence, encountered
throughout all creation. Our selves are made of God's self. But this
does not mean that the world is our creation, or that we are God. It
does mean that this awareness, this sense of uniqueness we feel cannot possibly have come just from ourselves. It is bigger than us and
must be in everyone else. In all living things. In stones and water
and fire. Everywhere. Indeed, this sense of self, this *Anochi*, is so
holy we correctly intuit that it has created us. We live and breathe
through its radiance and compassion. It is the source of our vital

energy. And we are fulfilled through its service. Even as we secretly suspect that through making this one Self a conscious reality, history will at last be resolved into one C-major chord, the entire Torah pronounceable as one long uninterrupted Name of God.

SELF-AWARENESS

Self is orchestration of our awareness, the integration of consciousness, what holds it all together, makes it whole and able to be called by a single name—our name. Self is what integrates and unifies our physical body, our thoughts, our actions. And it is the same with God and creation.

The universe too has a name by which it means to integrate its myriad contradictions into one organism. The universe, like you and I, has a self, a self that nourishes and sustains each individual self. God is to being as the Self is to us. God is the *Anochi shel Olam*, the "I" of the world, the Self of the Universe.

In the word of the philosopher and physician Moses Maimonides writing in the twelfth century, not only is God "the one who knows [and] that which is known [God is also]...the knowing itself."[5]

Or, as Nachman of Bratslav observed:

> The essence of a person is consciousness and therefore wherever one is conscious, there is the whole person. And likewise one who knows and attains an understanding of God is actually in God. The greater a person's knowing, the more that person is included in the Root, in God.[6]

One of my high school students once asked me if I could prove there was a God. Instead I asked her if she had a self. She thought for a moment and said, "Of course."

"And is your self important to you?"

"Very," she replied.

"And where would you be," I pushed, "without your self?"

"In big trouble."

"Can you prove you have one?"

She smiled. "I get what you mean."

The essence of spirituality is a return to the self, a re-direction of vision of the one who asks the question, an almost serendipitous discovery that what is sought is, and has always been, right here all along. "It," in other words, is never somewhere else. Could this stubborn insistence that God has no body whatsoever be another way of keeping this primary and holy truth alive? If God has no body, then God is nowhere. And I need go nowhere.

Spirituality is always in reference to two "I"s, the "i" of the person and the "I" of the Universe. It is religion in a personal mode, religion from the point of view of the "i" of yourself and from the point of view of the "I" of the Universe. Spirituality is personal immediacy and the immediacy of God's presence. Most of the time it is very quiet, so quiet that it could be drowned out by the slightest noise or lost to the slightest distraction. Indeed God's presence already permeates all creation. We name it when we are born with our first cry and whisper it as we die with our last breath. It wants only to be made tangible through our hands.

We are agents, instruments of God's presence. We are not at odds with the Self of the Universe; we are part of it. And to be aware of this is to give our lives ultimate meaning and purpose. To realize that we are servants, through everything that we do, with or without our consent, is to be able to do anything; it is our empowerment and fulfillment. Spirituality is a dimension of living where we are aware of God's presence. It is being concerned with how what we do affects God and how what God does affects us.

Self-Reflection at Sinai

SINAI IS THE STORY OF A TIME WHEN, for just a moment, we became aware of our own awareness. Self-conscious of our own conscious-ness. The light of the first verses of Genesis is a metaphor for the dawning of human awareness.[7] In one sense, all of Scripture is the story of the discovery of and straying from that light. But, until Sinai, the light was unaware of itself: a child who did not know it could see. Not until the mountain did we become conscious of the medium by which we are conscious. Vision was turned back into itself, creating the momentary sensation of blindness. The light must have been too bright, for we said, "Let not God speak to us, lest we die." (Exodus 20:16)

And later, even the One of Being confides in Moses, the trans-lator, that "a human being shall not see My face and live." (Exodus 33:20) Awareness may not behold itself while it is in the act of be-holding itself. Could a fish learn of how fishes swim in water by watching them from dry land—unless, of course, it was in the few twitching moments before its death? Could we, as Franz Rosenzweig, the German philosopher, asked, take out our eyes to see how we see? No. Immediacy may not reflect upon immediacy and remain both itself and in the present.

"You shall not see My face and live." If you are willing to die, then perhaps we can do business. But as long as you hang on to your ego, your selfhood, going around being a subject, comprehend-ing other subjects and thereby making them objects, you will not see Me.

Here might lie the meaning of God's strange reply to Moses at Sinai: "After I pass, I shall remove my hand and you can see My back." (Exodus 33:23) On a literal, anthropomorphic level, it is obviously nonsense; but if we consider it as Moses' discovery that immediacy cannot be self-reflective, that consciousness cannot turn back upon itself, then a new understanding emerges. Especially if we remember that the Hebrew word *achorai*, "*My back*," also has a temporal sense. "The best you can hope for," God tells Moses, "is to see what it is like just after I have been there." Is this not the fate of any religious person—to perpetually stand awestruck! Contemplating the One who can only be met in the present but comprehended in the past tense. We cannot know God in the future. And, as we have seen, immediacy is out of the question. But, "When I remove my hand, you will be able to see My back."

This Sinai story of how we once endured the self-reflection of our own consciousness tells that there are not one, but two parts: two modes of becoming conscious. You will recall that there were two sets of commandments. The first set was either withdrawn or smashed. According to one legend, when God gave the commandments, everyone died. The One of Being apparently did not yet know that human beings could not look upon Being face-to-face and live. So God took the commandments back. And everyone came back to life. According to the other, more popular legend, the bargain between God and Israel was terminated by Moses when he broke the tablets in anger over the business with the calf. But, in either case, the first attempt on the part of the Holy One to covenant with Israel failed. In other words, the first try at fathoming our own awareness fails. There is some dying or shattering in between. And then, the second set is given and received without much fuss at all. Which leads us to suspect that, since death and brokenness are still so frequent, the second giving (coming!) has not happened. That the second set has not yet been given and that all we possess are the broken fragments of the first set, which were nevertheless also carried in the ark. (*Berakhot* 8b) Imagine it: a sacred chest filled with shattered words and pieces of stone. We live in a time after the confusion of trying to endure the self-reflection of our own consciousness, but before we have succeeded.

The bush in its pristine loneliness is a prototype and a prophecy of the mountain yet to come. There are some things one sees that, like the bush, "consume" all of a person and demand only that he soon return, bringing as many others as he can along with him. The great paradigm within the Western myth of self-awareness is the public spectacle of a few years later at Sinai; even as Elijah's own lonely hearing of the "still small voice" is an echo or a memory of that same Sinai event generations later. It keeps happening. The bush and the slaves and Moses and Elijah are all present within one another and you and me. Some scholars have even suggested that, at the historical time of the going out from Egypt, the idea of individuated selves that we know today did not exist. There was only the corporate body of the people. Their experience of revelation was as a whole people. God may have "spoken" to one organism! In which case it may have been, as it is today, one against one. This one against the One.

The Source of the Voice

Each age must in its turn recall this memory of how we have sought to become aware of our own consciousness, and understand it for itself. For each age looks back on the event and sees a different problem. For us, the question is not so much one of whether or not Spirit speaks, but from whence comes its voice.

Within the Western religions of revelation, everything depends on the source of the Voice. If it comes from beyond people, then there is a God. If it comes from within them, then there is no God.

The Orthodox claim "He" spoke once and for all at Sinai—but that we were all there to hear it. The point is that God is more than us, other than us, different from us, beyond us, outside us. If humanity ceased to be, the voice would still sound though no one would be there to hear. In either case, with or without people to listen, the documents of revelation can at least in principle be records of God's truth. This is the key point: The Holy One is more than us. And since God's voice issues from the outside, it instructs, chastens, and commands. Since the voice is exclusively from outside, God is wholly other than us.

If on the other hand, as liberals claim, the voice comes from within, then the spiritual enterprise is inverted. Religion is inescapably humanism. It makes little difference here whether the voice from within is heard as (divine) inspiration, conscience, insight, or intuition. What matters is that if all people were to vanish from the earth, the voice would surely disappear with them. Since the voice is exclusively from the inside, there is no God but humanity.

There are, of course, more complicated versions of these two choices. God might, in fact, be beyond us but only speak through us. Or, conversely, God might only be a human invention whose voice is projected outwards and then reflected back from the heavens. But, in either case, the final question remains: What is the real source of the voice?

Philosopher Emil Fackenheim once wisely suggested that, if an agnostic had been present at Mount Sinai, he would have heard the thunder and seen the lightning but wondered what all the commotion was about. To which we might add that, had we been there, we would have doubtless been paralyzed by our inability to decide whether the voice came from outside or inside ourselves—when, of course, it is clear now that the choice itself is spurious. For the voice, if it be truly the voice of the Holy One of Being, speaks from both without and within. And it is the same voice.

THE REVELATION OF SILENCE

At the time of teaching, it is the teacher who—by some word or deed, a question, a blow, or simply through silence—forces the student to hear a voice that comes from within. All genuine learning is thus the self's disclosure to itself. The voice issues with such clarity that the ones who learn refuse to believe that it is their own. Insisting instead that it has come from the teacher who is across the room. All the great teachers share this alert passivity. A guide who is willing to draw out of the novice an innermost self, and who will remain long enough for a student to step back and discover what he or she has thought all along, or said, or done.

How odd and yet how universal the misconception, on the part of all who would learn, that the knowledge they seek is outside them. To what lengths we go geographically, financially, and spiritually to find someone who will enable us to hear our own inner voice. At Sinai everyone is a student and all hear the voice of the Teacher. Not only is it a clear, publicly audible, external voice; it is also a voice that is the sound of our own breathing, a very precious, alert silence.

Among the Hasidim, the Eastern European spiritual revivalists of the eighteenth and nineteenth centuries, the word "Torah" acquired meaning beyond the Five Books of Moses or even beyond a symbol of God's revelation to humanity. It began to refer to a master's teaching, particularly the oral teaching delivered at the table during a holy meal. The rabbi would "say Torah." In principle, there were as many different "Torahs" as there were teachers. And while it is true that many teachings began with a verse from Scripture—that is, God's Torah—it is clear that there was no certain agreement or unanimity of these variegated teachings. Each rebbe had his own central and unique teaching. His own Torah. In other words, the One of Being utters a word that initiates revelation, even as we create ourselves by giving utterance to our own.

And this is, if you will permit, my Torah: that our own frequent reachings into that river of light that nourishes our psyche is our Torah. What we think and joke and muse—when we really tell the truth—*that* is our Torah. And God, then, is not so much a speaker from the outside or a whisper from within, but the One on account of whom we hear "I am…" And the medium of that revelation is silence. Rabbi Abahu taught in the name of Rabbi Yohanan that when God said, "I am," no creature uttered a sound. Even the sea did not move. There was a deafening silence throughout the world. Only then did the voice issue. (*Shemot Rabba* 29:9) So it is with all teaching.

And we come again to the paradox of any sustained spiritual search. A voice that speaks from the highest heavens and a voice from the inner chambers of the self. How could this possibly be? How could God who is infinite speak with people who are finite and not destroy them both? How could a bush burn and not be consumed? "Let not the Lord talk to us lest we die!" (Exodus 20:16). How could consciousness behold itself in the very moment of its consciousness? How can the eye behold itself? It is all the same. And sooner or later all religious traditions must confront the impossible logic. (Indeed, their solution to that problem will determine the form their religion will take.) That what was without shall merge with what was within. Here is the common idea that all varieties of religion share. It is a kind of primary human experience toward which both science and religion converge. The Bible's image for the resolution of all paradox is the coming of the Messiah. The final transformation of consciousness itself. The Baal Shem Tov explained it this way: "The coming of the Messiah does not depend upon anything supernatural, but rather upon human growth and self-transformation…. The world will only be transformed…when people realize that the Messiah is not someone wholly other than themselves."[8]

The more we become aware, the more we realize that we are in everything and everything is in us. The One we call the Holy One, and the ones the Holy One calls us, are the same beings, seen from different sides. So it is only natural that the voice be heard to issue from different directions. The question is not "Who makes who real?", whether people are making God or God is making people—for both make each other come to be. Both are One. *Yehido shel Olam*. The Only One of the Universe.

And our refusal to realize this, our inability to make it real, may just be the reason that the "anointed One" tarries. Surely the word would then break forth from children and their grandparents. From hewers of wood to the most erudite sages. From the first person to the last person. From even you and me. Protoplasm and consciousness aware of their common source.

PREVIOUSLY PUBLISHED IN
UNION OF AMERICAN HEBREW CONGREGATIONS'
TORAT HAYIM: LIVING TORAH, 1997

It's All God

"MAKE ME A SANCTUARY that I may dwell among them." (Exodus 25:8) That pretty much sums up the religious enterprise: You have to do something, so that God, who is not there, can be. The tabernacle is a metaphor for the religion we "construct," an exercise we perform to alter our consciousness.

Or, to put it another way: If God's everywhere, then why can't we find God anywhere? If God made the world and, as Menachem Nahum of Chernobyl teaches, the presence of the Creator is within each created thing, then why can't we find it? We have this nagging suspicion that God is ubiquitous; we just can't seem to find God.

According to Shneur Zalman of Lyadi (d. 1813), it's not that there is a world and God is everywhere within it. It's that there is God and the world is everywhere within God. There is nothing, absolutely nothing, that is not already God. It's all God. You, me, the trees, the murders, the children, the sewers, the blossoms of springtime, the toxic waste dumps, the tabernacle—it's all God. At the end of Job, God says, in effect, I'm the whole kazoo. Not just the sunshine and bluebirds, but even in the lions tearing gazelles, vultures eating carrion. Everything. Everywhere. God. God. God.

And how do you get to that awareness? It has something to do with how you behave as a human being. Being a decent human being increases the chances that you'll find it, that it'll dawn on you, just as being a louse gradually seals you off from it. It's not that you're religious to be good; it's that you're good to be religious!

But suppose you want this awareness more of the time: that it's all God, that the presence of the Creator is everywhere. Suppose

* existing or being everywhere at the same time

you say, I want to be aware of the presence of the Creator more than just sporadically. What do I do? That's where religion comes in. That's where constructing the tabernacle takes over. Religion, you might say, is the collected advice of those who have come before us on how to attain it. Sure it doesn't always work. Sure it can easily be perverted. But the "hit rate" is way ahead of what ever is in second place. So God says (Exodus 25:8), "You build me this sacred place, just as I've told you, so that I can dwell among you." Whenever you perform a religious deed with devotion and reverence, then you get it. Every time. It's all God.

ORIGINALLY PUBLISHED IN
MEDITATION FROM THE HEART OF JUDAISM, 1997

Silencing the Inner Voice(s)

"IF WE HAD A KEEN VISION and feeling for all ordinary human life, it would be like hearing the grass grow, the squirrel's heart beat, and we should die of that roar which lies on the other side of silence."—George Eliott

My favorite part of sailing comes about fifteen minutes into the voyage, after we've loaded all our gear aboard, removed all the covers, freed all the neatly coiled lines, pumped the bilges, checked the safety equipment, opened the seacocks, turned "on" the batteries, hoisted the "iron Genoa" (started the engine), cast off the mooring line, negotiated our way through the maze of boats in the harbor, raised the main, unfurled the jib, trimmed the sails, set a course— then the moment comes. I reach down to the throttle and pull it backward all the way, back past "idle," and shut off the fuel to the diesel. It takes a second or two to take effect. The engine obediently chugs and sputters to a stop. Now, except for the whisper of the wind in the sails and the gurgle of water rushing past the hull, there is only silence. There's nothing to say. Indeed, to say anything would damage the serenity of the moment. We are better at making noise than enduring silence. But silence is better than noise. Attaining silence may just be the reason for prayer. But I don't mean just not talking. I mean also stilling the inner dialogue. And, as in so much Jewish spirituality, this is taught through a careful examination of sacred text.

We have a fascinating irregularity in Numbers 7:89. After all the princes of Israel have brought their gifts of consecration, Moses is left alone in the newly completed wilderness tabernacle. The text reads: "[Moses] heard the Divine Voice speaking to him...." Given the context, that does not seem especially noteworthy at all. A very close reading however turns up one extraneous dot. Normally the word for speaking, *midabbaer*, appears in the *piel* conjugation with a dot, or *dagesh*, in the middle root letter. But curiously here, in addition to the one in the *beit*, the *dalet* is also vocalized with a *dagesh* of its own. And, if the conjugation is *piel*, that dot is *not* supposed to be there.

Rashi, the great Medieval commentator, catches the irregularity and explains that our verb, *midabbaer*, is actually an odd form of what used to be *mitdabaer*, a *hitpael* with an assimilated letter *hay*. All that remains of the *hay* is the *dagesh*. And all this now renders the verse not "[Moses] heard the Divine Voice speaking to him," but reflexively: "He heard the Voice uttering itself." Moses overheard the Divine Self uttering itself! That you can enter a place and overhear the Self of the Universe uttering itself. But if the Divine Self is uttering itself and the Divine Self is also the source of yourself, then who is listening?

SPEAKER OF THE SELF

Did you ever talk to yourself? I don't mean when you were alone in the car. I mean: Did you ever ask yourself a question to find out if you knew the answer? Like, "Who am I?" or "What is the meaning of my life?" Did you ever get an answer? What would you do if the answer were: "Who wants to know?" In other words: When you talk to yourself, who's talking and who's listening?

One of the discontents of civilization is the split between who we are and who is speaking. We are afflicted with a generic schizophrenia, disjunctive personalities. Call it the reflexive self: some other person living in there. A piece of consciousness broken off from awareness. And the fact that we can hold these interior conversations with our "selves" means that we are fragmented, alienated, broken.

If we were whole, then there could be no conversation, because there would be no one else in there to talk to.

I am convinced that such self-reflecting mind games are the enemy of religious experience. In the cinema, this is called "breaking the third wall." The actor suddenly turns to the camera and speaks to it as if it were a real person, jarring the viewers into realizing they are only watching a movie. The spell is broken.

The Hasidic rebbe Menachem Mendl of Kotzk deliberately misreads Deuteronomy 5:5, in which Moses says, "*Anochi omed bayn Adonai u'vaynaykhem*," "I stood between God and you." Menachem Mendl teaches: it is your I, "your ego that stands between you and God. Normally not even an iron barrier can separate Israel from God, but self-preoccupation and ego will drive them apart."[9]

In other words, when we do something with all of us, we're not aware we're doing it. There is no one *in there* to hear it. The part of our consciousness that normally tells the rest of us that we are present is busy doing it too. As Buckaroo Bonzai said: "Wherever you go, there you are."

DANCING ON THE ROPE

My daughter once told me that the way to know I was dancing was to dance with so much of me that I stopped worrying about what I looked like on the dance floor. I told her that if she looked the way I did when I danced, she'd worry too. But she only said that in order to really dance, you must give yourself to the music. "Let it tell you what to do; quit being so self-conscious. The only way you will ever know you have danced, Daddy, is if, once the music has stopped, you realize you didn't know you were dancing."

This reminds me of a story told of Rabbi Hayim of Krosno, a disciple of the Baal Shem Tov. He once stopped with his students to watch a man dance on a rope strung high between two buildings. Rabbi Hayim became so absorbed in the spectacle that his Hasidim asked him what he found so fascinating in such a frivolous circus performance.

"I can't get over it," he explained. "This man is risking his life, and I am not sure why. I am sure that while he is walking on the rope, he cannot be thinking about the hundred gulden he is earning; he cannot be thinking about the step he has just taken or the step he is going to take next; he cannot even be thinking about where he is: If he did, he would fall to his death. He must be utterly unaware of himself!'"[10]

When we're "dancing on the rope," the inner conversation ceases and we realize that our sense of self is actually an obstacle. It splits us in two; renders us observers of our own lives; tricks us into thinking that our self is somehow other than who we are. There is only one of you in there and out here, and it's the same one. And the business of serious religion is to get you to abolish the distinctions between inside and outside, observer and observed. The goal is to be fully present in whatever you do, just like God is in the world.

WANTING WHAT GOD WANTS

"If mysticism is the quintessence of religion," then, as Moshe Idel opines in his book, *Kabbala: New Perspectives*, "the quintessence of mysticism is the sense of union with God."[11] In Judaism, "union with God" is called *devekut*, or, literally, "cleaving." The classic sources of *devekut* are Deuteronomy 4:4: "But you that cleave [*had'vaykim*] unto the Lord your God this day are alive everyone of you this day"; and Isaiah 43:11: "*Anochi Adonai anochi*, I, I am the Lord," where the first "I" is God and the second is the self. Now the famous line at the burning bush, "*Ehyeh asher ehyeh*," of Exodus 3:14, means, "I will be who you are!"

We don't want to just read about what God wants. We don't want someone else telling us what God wants either. We don't even want God telling us what God wants. We want our eyes to be God's eyes so that we can see the world the way God sees it. We want our teaching to be God's Torah. We want our hands to do God's work. We want our prayers to be God's prayers. We want to want what God wants. *Devekut*: being one with God.

Idel identifies three forms of *devekut*.[12] First comes what he calls Aristotelian *devekut*. I would call it cognitive *devekut*. In this form of union, during the act of cognition the knower and the known become one. A second mode of *devekut*, Idel terms the theurgic. I would call it the *devekut* of behavior. In this experience, the Jew seeks to literally affect God through specific actions. In this mode of *devekut*, your will and your very deeds become God's. If you become a servant of God, then your action is God's action. By repairing things here, we repair them above. A personality drawn to such *devekut* is action oriented, content neither with study nor with meditation. This person is a doer, an achiever, a fixer, someone who wants to repair the world. Seekers of the last form of *devekut* are primarily concerned with the re-uniting of the soul with its root. They draw heavily on the imagery of transformation, ascent, and return. I would call it the *devekut* of prayer. The focus of this third personality is neither cerebral or behavioral, but emotional. Such a soul is drawn to closing his eyes, losing herself in song, sitting in silence.

THE ONE WHO ASKS IS THE ONE WHO HEARS

We can now reconsider the strange case of the extra *dagesh* in Numbers 7:89, and the question with which we began of how to stop being self-conscious. In the words of Nachman of Bratslav: "The core of a human being is his consciousness. Where one's consciousness is, there is the whole person. Thus one who knows and reaches an understanding of the divine is really in the divine. The greater one's knowing, the more fully is he included in his root in God."[13]

I am convinced that *devekut* is more than being one with God. *Devekut* is a theological metaphor for stopping the dialogue between the two inner voices, for self-unification. *Devekut* is a time when the outer person is revealed to be illusory, a figment of the language, an iron barrier separating us from God. Now only an unselfconscious awareness remains, an awareness that bears a wonderful similarity to the Divine. On Yom Kippur, a woman in my congregation offered a personal prayer in which she prayed for the wisdom to "wish to be who she was."

Devekut is when the one who asks and the one who hears become the same. We realize to our embarrassment that we have been who we were all along and that it was only linguistic convention that tricked us into thinking we were someone else. We cannot make God do what we want, but in thinking, doing, and praying what God wants, we become one with God and with ourselves. I will be who we are, I even I.

Hershey with Almonds

WHEN KAREN WAS PREGNANT with our second child, we lived in a little shoebox of an apartment in the town of Marlborough outside of Boston. In the dead of winter and the middle of the night, she awakened me with a confession.

"Larry, I know this sounds crazy, but I would give anything for a chocolate bar, especially one with almonds."

I knew at once that this was the mythic "strange craving" of a pregnant woman. Before she could even call it a request, I jumped out of bed, pulled my Levi's on over my pajamas, a sweatshirt, then my snow parka, boots, hat, gloves.

"Don't worry about a thing, sweetheart," I said. (After all, she'd been carrying our child around in her belly now for six months. This was the least I could do.)

When I got downstairs, I realized that it had been snowing for a few hours. The car was covered with a few inches of heavy, wet slush. But only after I had managed to clean it off did it dawn on me: Where would I find a chocolate bar in Marlborough, Massachusetts, in the middle of the night, in a blizzard? And then it hit me: of course, at the Holiday Inn out on I-495.

The night clerk watched incredulously as a man in pajamas and snow parka skidded to a stop under the portico, ran inside, punched quarters into the candy machine, waved, and drove off into the snowstorm.

I presented my offering. Karen was a little embarrassed, but unequivocally grateful. As for me, I learned something precious about myself. I normally have a well-developed ego, but for about forty-five minutes twenty years ago, I did not have an ego of my own. Instead, I was only an extension of Karen Kushner's ego. Instead of doing what I wanted and remaining in a warm bed, I did what she wanted and drove around in the middle of the night in a blizzard looking for a chocolate bar.

And here's the amazing part. It made me happier to do what my wife wanted than to do what I wanted. By letting go of my ego, I was happier than if I had tried to please myself. By doing what your lover wants, you transcend yourself. So it is with all sacred deeds. We give ourselves over to them, humbly offer ourselves as servants of something or someone greater. In so doing, we are transformed.

ORIGINALLY PUBLISHED IN
MY PEOPLE'S PRAYER BOOK, VOL. 2, 1998

"Open My Lips"

IT SEEMS ODD THAT AS A PRELUDE to the central rubric of Jewish liturgy, the *Amida*—a bouquet of prayers of praise, petition, and thanksgiving—the most intensely conversational script of the entire prayerbook, someone thought to throw in a Psalm 51:17: "God, open my lips so that my mouth may declare Your praise."

Wouldn't it make more sense to say something like, "Here I am God, ready to begin our conversation," or "Permit me to introduce myself," or "I know we haven't always seen eye to eye on certain things," something that would accentuate the dialogic nature of what will follow. For there to be a conversation, an intercession, there must be two discrete parties. It takes two to tango.

In much (but not all) of the Hebrew Bible and the prayerbook, God and people are separate, distinct, discrete, autonomous, independent, and apart from one another. God says this, we say that. God does this, we do that. God's there, we're here. The energy of the whole thing comes precisely from our being separate from one another. So why begin our personal prayers with a denial of that mutual autonomy and free will?

The psalm says, "God, would you please open my mouth." Hey, who's working my mouth anyway, me or God? Who's praising God, me or God? What's going on here?

What's going on here is another spiritual paradigm, one in which God and people are not only not distinct from one another but are literally within one another. God is the ocean and we are the waves. In the words of the Hasidic maxim, *"Alles is Gott,"* "It's all God." My mouth is God's mouth. My praises are God's words. In

Rabbi Kalnoymos Kalmish Shapira of Piesetzna's words, "Not only does God hear our prayers, God prays them through us as well!"

The words of the *Amida* that will follow may sound like they come from me, but in truth they come from a higher source. Prayer may ultimately be an exercise for helping us let go of our egos, hopelessly anchored to this world where one person is discrete from another and from God, and soar to the heavens where we realize there is a holy One to all being and that we have been an expression of it all along. "God, open my lips so that my mouth may declare Your praise."

Eyes
Remade for Wonder

AT ANY GIVEN MOMENT, YOU CAN ONLY BE WHERE YOU ARE. You can wish to be somewhere else, but that will only decrease the likelihood you'll succeed. You get somewhere else by first realizing and accepting where you are and who you are.

There are a series of bumper stickers that say things like "I'd rather be fishing" or "I'd rather be playing golf." The other day I saw a new one. It said: "I'd rather be here now." That strikes me as wise and terribly religious. What we seek is not somewhere else. It (whatever "it" be) is right here and right now. Go ahead, feel it in the effortless emptying and filling of your lungs, the moisture on your tongue, the involuntary blinking of your eyes. Right there! Now that may not be the end, but it is surely and inescapably the beginning. But how, once you find it, to stay there, even for a moment or so, is not so easy.

There is an almost mythic scene in the movie *Titanic* when the great ship is going down and the band plays on. But the director, James Cameron, added one line that changes everything. The musicians, with their fellow passengers running about in hopeless helter-skelter, decide to go on playing anyway. (What else is there to do?) As they are about to begin to play what will probably be their last song, one of them (I think it was a violinist) reflects for a moment and then says to his colleagues, "Gentlemen, it has been an honor to play with you." It occurs to me that that may just be all any of us ever get to say—not in futility, or with the grim awareness that all is lost, but with the knowledge that at any given moment, we are where we are and we can choose to run around in senseless panic or accept our destiny with dignity and, yes, even gratitude.

"It has been an honor to play with you." In so doing, we transform disaster, if not into success, then at least into dignity, sweetness, and meaning. Isn't that the goal of any would-be religion: to return us to where we are with a renewed sense of gratitude? To simply be fully present, with eyes remade for wonder…

The Letter Ayin

AYIN DOES NOT SPEAK. It only sees. It is an eye, *ayin*. Close your eyes. Open your mouth. Now try to see. That is the sound of *ayin*. It is the silent humility of *anavah* of serving the Master of the Universe. Serving. Worshiping *avodah*. Emptying yourself so that you can be filled with God.

But not all who serve, serve the living God. To *ayin* also belongs the *ayin* of the golden calf, *agel,* and the *ayin* of the perverse service of a fetish of an idol, *avodah zara.* This is the *ayin* of slavery that shames: "*Avadim ha-yinu,* We were slaves…"

But there is also an *ayin* of service that frees. The great collar, the yoke, *ohl,* by which the ox serves his master is not his shame but his fulfillment. This is the purpose for which you were set on this earth: to serve God. To take upon yourself the yoke of the Kingdom of Heaven.

This is why the Ten Commandments, the ten utterances, *aseret ha-dibrot,* which tell us how to begin to serve are *ayin* begun. And the holy books that tell you how our parents have served are also *ayin, aytz chayim.* They are a tree of life. "It is a tree of life for those who hold on to it."

The Amnesia of Unio Mysticia

BEING *AT ONE* WITH THE HOLY ONE OF BEING is not about becoming the same as God but about forgetting the boundaries of self. You forget, at least for a moment, the mind game of where you end and creation begins. You understand that you are an expression of creation: It is in you and you are everywhere in it.

There are many ways we reach for the Holy One(ness). We can attain self-transcendence through our mind in study, through our heart in prayer, or with our hands in sacred deed. We say, in effect, that through becoming God's agent, through voluntarily setting God's will above our own, we literally lose our selves and become One with the One whom we serve. It rarely lasts for more than a moment.

The primary obstacle to becoming one is self-awareness, self-consciousness, talking to oneself. And for this reason, high awareness involves stopping, ignoring, forgetting the conversation we routinely carry on inside our heads between different parts of our personalities. Such amnesia is another word for self-unification. When the one who asks and the one who hears are the same, we are who we are. We realize, to our embarrassment, that we have been ourselves all along and only linguistic convention tricked us into thinking that we were someone else. In thinking, praying, and doing what God wants, we become one with God and the Universe. The outer person is an illusion, a figment of language. Only an un-self-awareness remains.

Being Where You Are

A *SEFER TORAH* IS WRITTEN WITHOUT VOWELS. We have to fill them in mentally as we read. Someone who understands Hebrew and has a rough idea of the story can usually figure out the vowels. But occasionally a word appears that can be read in different ways, depending on the vowels we add.

Such a word occurs in Genesis 2:1. The letters *vav, yod, khaf, lammed, vav* are usually given certain vowels so that they are pronounced *vaye'khu-lu,* which means "were finished." Taken in this manner, the verse reads: "The heaven and the earth *were finished...*"

In the Talmud, however, Rabbi Hamnuna notices that, by adding different vowels, the letters *vav, yod, khaf, lammed, vav* could also be pronounced *vaye'kha-lu,* which means "and they finished." Taken in this manner, the verse reads: "*And they finished* the heaven and the earth." (*Shabbat* 119b)

This raises another question: Who were the "they" who finished the heaven and the earth? Rabbi Hamnuna says that the "they" refers to God and people. Not only do we help God by caring for and repairing creation, we also join God on the eve of every *Shabbat* by finishing our work.

Why is it so important to be finished? Perhaps because every unfinished task—yesterday's homework, household chores, someone we need to forgive, a hobby project—demands a piece of our attention. It wants us to be "back in yesterday," worrying about what we didn't finish, or it wants us to be "already in tomorrow," worrying about what we still need to do. And whenever we are "back in yesterday" or "already in tomorrow," we are not fully here. Our bodies are obviously present, but our attention is somewhere else.

To make *Shabbat*, we must, therefore, either finish our work, as God did, or say to ourselves, "Even if it's not done, I'm going to pretend it's done anyway. On *Shabbat*, I do not worry about what I didn't finish yesterday or what I must do tomorrow; I'm going to be right here. Each week, on *Shabbat* I will enjoy some special time, remaining where I am, opening my eyes to the wonder and miracle of creation."

Rabbi Isaac lived in the city of Cracow. He was very poor, so when he dreamed three times in a row about a great treasure buried under a bridge in the distant city of Prague, he set out on the journey to find it. When he arrived in Prague, he discovered that the place he had seen in the dream was patrolled day and night by the king's guards. He circled the spot, watching it from a distance until one day the guards noticed him. When the captain called to Rabbi Isaac and demanded to know what he was doing there, the rabbi told him about the dream.

"You mean to tell me that you believe in such dreams!" laughed the captain. "If I believed in them, I would have to go all the way to Cracow and find some rabbi, named Isaac, because I have dreamed that a great treasure lies buried beneath his bed!" Rabbi Isaac thanked the captain, returned home, pushed aside his bed, and dug up the treasure that had been there all along.

What we are seeking is not in the past or in the future. It is not far away or in the possession of someone else. It is exactly where we are, and every seventh day, on *Shabbat*, the miracles of creation can be ours.

Higher Worlds

THERE ARE HIGHER HOLIER WORLDS than this one.
Obviously no one can know how many there are.
Nor can we be certain
That a certain rung of holy awareness
Is the same for different persons.
We only know that most of the time,
We are busy here below the bottom one.
And that above the top one is the Nameless One,
The one named *Ayn Sof,* the One without end.
And that the One comes down to us, as it were,
Like light poured down
Through some cascading waterfall.
And that we go up to the One
Through the same network,
Like salmon returning upstream to spawn.
But that whether like water down a fall
Or creatures swimming home,
By the time each reaches its destination
There is not much remaining.
Only a thin, diluted version of what once started out.
So that what we see of the One here is dim.
And what the One sees of us on high,
While very true to what we really are,
Might not look the way we do
To each other.

But in any case, ordinary souls, like you and I, are the links between this world and the higher ones, shuttling back and forth, carrying buckets of light in our heads.

> Now these channels
> Through which God and people commute to each other
> Are understood by many analogies.
> Each of them are but one
> Of the infinite number of ways
> Of representing the meeting
> With the Holy One.
> The ascent of souls.
> And yet each is accurate:

In the heavens above there are palaces or *hechalot*: Lush meadows, chambers like valleys, awaiting the traveler. Each room brighter than the one before.

Each person is a unique replica of the primordial human, *Adam Kadmon*. And this archetype is also the body of the universe. A manifestation of consciousness in the shape of a person. "...with light streaming from the apertures in his face..."

The creation of the world is a metaphor for the emergence of awareness. So that returning to our genesis, be it cosmic to the furthest reaches of the heavens or microscopic to sub-atomic particles, leads likewise through concentric spheres of increasing /decreasing size. There are ten modes of awareness.

Human consciousness, inner spiritual space, can likewise be set in a diagram. The map will suggest the paradox of encountered reality and the balance within the human soul. It must therefore also have an axis of symmetry. A right side and a left side. Masculine and feminine. It will intimate that there are ever increasing spheres above and ever diminishing spheres within. It will be in the shape of a person. Or it will be like a family tree that can either suggest how one's progenitors conspired to make one man or how one person conspired to populate the universe. In other words a tree on which you place yourself as the seed of the root or the bud on the uppermost branch.

The drawing might also be envisioned as the process whereby the Holy One created man. Or whereby souls reach towards an awareness of their Creator. And thus the image will suggest how we and God are connected through a network of channels. Drawn to one another through their mutual need to reunite. The expression of which we understand to be the Torah.

This world.
The one in which you are reading these words
Is at the center of concentric worlds.
They are each bigger than this place.
They are higher.
Holier and more real than this world.

Shabbos is more real than Wednesday.
Jerusalem is more real than Chicago.
The *sukka* is more real than a garage.
Tsadaka is more real than income tax.
Holy is more real than profane.
Standing closer to the Holy One is more real
than being far from the Holy One.
But they are also smaller than this ordinary world.
For they are within it.

There are many degrees of holiness. Perhaps as described by the school of Rabbi Isaac Luria, the great sixteenth century Kabbalist: Doing, Formation, Creation, and Emanation. Or perhaps as we read elsewhere, "The world was created with ten words" There are ten *sefirot,* or spheres, or worlds. Or 310 worlds, *shai olamot,* hinted at in the final *mishna* of *Uktsin.*

Spiritual journeys can only be chronicled, not reported. What we speak of once we have returned are like stories from our childhood or legends from of old.

While you can speak of higher worlds from within lower ones with seeming accuracy, you can really only comprehend a higher world from within it.

We are mistaken to imagine that we can share the understanding of higher worlds with those who have remained behind. This is because the awareness of holier worlds shatters the earthenware vessels unable to withstand the light. To try to speak of the Holy One in the language of this world is already to speak of something else other than the Holy One.

Each world has a logic unique to it. In this world, for instance, the logic of Aristotle dominates. Nothing can be its opposite.

When we try to speak of what we have learned from a higher world, the logic from that place we bring down with us betrays us and we sound illogical. For instance, while it is true that this world is at the center and higher ones encircle out from it, it is also true that the highest world is the center and that this world is on the outermost periphery.

The levels of ascent might be represented alternatively with the Infinite One being at the center of introspection, or with the Infinite One being at the farthest reaches of the cosmos. But they are both the same. Even as the diagrams of the ten *sefirot* and the form of *Adam Kadmon,* the primordial man, are but different ways of representing the same thing. All manifestations of the Holy King.

This is the way you will go to higher worlds. You will pay great attention to the most trivial matters. Their great subtlety makes them elusive to most people who are too anxious to get on with things.

Allow yourself to dwell as if forever on the very first thought, for instance. The one you quickly gloss over since it is surely impossible, lascivious, preposterous, or silly. Yes. *That* is the one. To dwell—even for a moment—on the tiniest, most unlikely thought is the beginning.

Organized religion is our attempt to keep visions of other worlds present in this one. And this is why the religious endeavor tangles us in self-contradiction. For to speak of the other world in the language of this world is impossible.

Judaism focuses on the point where the two worlds meet: Sinai. And on the inscrutable record of that encounter: Torah. We seem to gain our invitation to the holy world by virtue of our presence there at that awesome mountain. Because the Jew is a member of a community who was present when the other world flooded this one with meaning, we are able to return as often as we wish, simply by remembering.

The Loving Star

Since Lev's birth, six months ago, everyone's position in the family has obviously undergone profound change. We have all had to do some adjusting as a new soul began to take his place in our family system. The children especially were worried whether or not there would still be enough love to go around and took to quarrelling even more than usual. And then I came up with this idea.

On a piece of paper with everyone watching on, I drew a figure with five circles, each one joined to all the others by channels.

There was much excitement. "Daddy, what is it?" But, I just went on drawing. Then in each circle I wrote the name of one of our family. Then I drew arrows, pointed in both directions extending between each person and everyone else in the family. I explained to everyone that the arrows were lines of loving and that the more love someone "put out" into the system—since every channel flowed in two directions but also sooner or later led back to itself—the more one "got back." I wrote at the top, "The loving always comes back to you" and at the bottom, "You can't take loving, you can only give loving." And I titled it, "The Kushner Family Loving Star." We taped it to the wall at a young one's eye level.

Every now and then I notice that one of the children is quietly studying the star. They trace the lines with their finger. Somehow drawing some reassurance from the drawing's truth.

Is that not the great childhood problem—and therefore the great human problem: to learn that it is good for you when other people love other people besides you? That I have a stake in their love. That I get more when others give to others.

That if I hoard it,
I lose it.
That if I give it away,
I get it back.

In Henry Miller's words: "Not to possess power but to radiate it." Perhaps it is not accidental that the ancient Kabbalistic diagrams that chart the worlds of holier reality above and within portray the flow of being as capable of moving in both directions. Perhaps there is an organic interconnectedness between each world. A kind of inevitable homeostatic balance.

In much the same way as in the human body/psyche.
We read in the morning prayers
"Blessed are You Lord our God, King of the Universe,
Who has formed people in wisdom.
Who created in each of us a life system
of organs and openings.
And when we are before Your Throne we know

That were one closed that should be open or
That were one open that should be closed,
Life could no longer go on.
And we would no longer be able
to stand in Your presence.
Blessed are You Lord
who heals us with miracles." (Daily Prayerbook)

This overflowing radiance
These emanations
This holy light
Streams down from on High
fills us and raises us up
And we reciprocate by permitting
The same holy light within us
To travel upward
"And holy messengers were going
up and down on it." (Genesis 28:12)

One of the kids wanted to know where God was on the "Kushner Family Loving Star," and after talking about it for a while we wrote the Hebrew letter *hay*—representing "God's Name"—in the very center of the star.

The Light of Creation

IN ORDER TO STUDY THE WORK OF CREATION we shall need to learn from humanity's two great truth traditions: science and religion. Their apparent disagreement is only the inevitable outcome of their different goals. Science tries to tell "what," and religion tries to answer "what for." As Houston Smith, the historian of religion, has suggested, it is the difference between quantification and qualification. Science is concerned with the empirical, objective, external fact, and religion with the personal, subjective, internal experience. Science must therefore "religiously" exclude feelings, while religion must "scientifically" factor them in. In classical science, the person of the observer can only contaminate, while in religion it is this same "person" who is our only concern. This explains why the results should on the surface appear so contradictory.

Science moves forward. Religion backward. Science grows by integrating more and more information into intelligible systems of increasing quantity and simplicity. Moving through its own eras, punctuated by revolutions, science grows by outgrowing the previous era's arrangements of information. Religion, on the other hand, eternally rediscovers the ancient truth known in principle by the first beings (or Being), which over the generations has become increasingly obscured, concealed, and encrusted. Until there is a revival (not a revolution). Some teacher or school or sect says, "We have forgotten the primary truth." In the words of my teacher, Arnold Jacob Wolf, "The old lies are true!"

Remember: One who is able to reach a rung of consciousness utterly unaware of oneself and aware only of the "outside world" (science), and one who is able to reach a rung of consciousness utterly unaware of the outside world and aware only of one's innermost self (spirit) will have arrived at the same place. In telling "what," one cannot avoid answering "why," just as in answering "why," one necessarily implicates "what." And so it is that the traditions are very close.

The opening chapter of Genesis is, for instance, restored to its proper place of "religion's" importance if we permit it to answer the question of the purpose of human existence or the meaning of life. As such, it is an eloquent answer to humanity's eternal "why?" It does not aim to offer a "scientific" account of creation. It is unconcerned with what actually happened. And yet, by teaching of the purpose of being, it betrays a surprisingly accurate, almost empirical, memory of events it could not have possibly witnessed.

THE POINT OF LIGHT

The first letter of the Hebrew Bible, *beit*, is the second letter of the Hebrew alphabet. The first letter of the alphabet, *aleph*, has virtually no sound at all. One might say, then, that there is nothing prior to the *beit* of creation. The letter *beit* itself, when prefixed to the beginning of a word, is a simple preposition meaning "in," "with," or "by." Now the first word of the Hebrew Bible, if we drop the first letter, *beit*, is *raysheet*, or, as it is commonly (but perhaps incorrectly) translated, "beginning." Variant traditions also render it as "Torah," in the sense of some preexistent wisdom or consciousness. One old festival prayerbook even has the Torah speak thus: "Long before any of His works, and long before the ancient things, I existed…when the world was water I existed; and while the world was chaos, I was then as a light.…" Hence we might now read the first verse of Genesis, "With Torah, God created the heavens and the earth.…" (*Bereshit Rabba* 1:1) But the Zohar is the most explicit:

> In the beginning—When the will of the King began to take effect, He engraved signs into the heavenly sphere that surrounded Him. Within the most hidden recess a dark flame issued from the mystery of *Ayn Sof*…neither white nor

black, neither red nor green, of no color whatever. Only after this flame began to assume size and dimension, did it produce radiant colors. From the innermost center of the flame sprang forth a well out of which colors issued and spread upon everything beneath....It could not be recognized at all until a hidden, supernal point shone forth....The primal center is the innermost light, of a translucence, subtlety, and purity beyond comprehension.... Beyond this point nothing can be known. Therefore it is called *raysheet*, beginning...[1] (I *Zohar* 15a)

This *raysheet* point rises from a soundless, almost *aleph*-like nothingness of infinite creative potential. It is none other than the beginning point of being. With *raysheet*, the Holy One fashioned the heavens and the earth. Being began.

During the second decade of this century, astronomer Edwin Hubble noticed that light reaching us from distant galaxies contained a disproportionate amount of longer wavelengths. This phenomenon of stretching out the wavelengths shifted their observable color along the spectrum toward the red. In the same way, the whine of a car approaching us on a highway sounds high-pitched and becomes lower as it moves away from us. This is because as the car approaches us, the sound waves are pushed together, resulting in a higher sound. As the car moves away from us, the sound waves are drawn apart, resulting in a lower sound. In the case of light, this bunching up, or shortening, of wavelengths makes the light bluer, and when drawn apart, or lengthened, they appear redder. This is called the Doppler shift. Hubble posited that, since distant galaxies are shifted toward the red, they must be moving away from us (and from one another): The universe is expanding. Everything is moving away from everything else at tremendous speed. At some specific time in the past, then, all the galaxies and stars and planets and, indeed, space itself must have been concentrated into a much denser mass.

We might therefore reconstruct the early hours and minutes of the universe. The closer or denser things would get, the hotter it would become. Only the simplest and most stable atoms could endure the intense temperature and radiation. This fact would also explain the great preponderance of simple hydrogen atoms to more complicated and less stable molecules in the universe.[2]

As we move further back in time, crossing the threshold where the temperature exceeds 4,000 degrees Kelvin, there would be so much radiation—pulsing waves of energy—that matter itself could not exist. There would instead be "only an ionized and undifferentiated soup…,"[3] an era of plasma.[4]

Here subatomic particles—leptons, hadrons, quarks, photons—could not stay together long enough even to form atoms. Instead, they would continually be created out of pure energy and, after short lives, be annihilated.[5] In this primordial furnace, the stuff of being began.

By the first 1/100 second, the universe was a hundred thousand million degrees centigrade with a density 4,000 million times that of water. A primeval fireball growing smaller and smaller and smaller. The immense gravity draws into itself all the matter and all the energy until, as it approaches infinite density, the curvature of space and time would likewise be infinite. Nothing escapes. All being is drawn back into one dimensionless mathematical point of infinite density, which Einstein would call a singularity. Not an object but an absurdity. A place where known physics comes to an end.[6] And, according to the midrash:

> We must suppress our thoughts and refrain from seeking and exploring what is above and below, what is before and what is beyond. Rabbi Johanan deduced this in Rabbi Levi's name from the fact that the first letter of the Torah is a *beit*, shaped like a three-sided square, the open side facing the direction of the following word. This teaches that just as the *beit* is closed on all sides and open on one side

only, so must you not inquire what is above or below (the universe), what was before creation and what will be after.[7]

Before the *beit* of *b'raysheet*, before the point of light, there was no before. For there was no time in which before could have been.

A HOVERING PRESENCE

The second verse of the creation legend speaks of void and nothingness. The universe was *tohu va-vohu*, primeval chaos. Darkness even darker than unconsciousness on the face of the abyss. But now the growing point of being's awareness begins to light up the blackness. The spirit of the Holy One hovers over the waters —like a dove fluttering over her nest. (*Hagigah* 15a and Rashi on Genesis 1:2) A soft hum filling the airless sky. Waiting there wanting only to become aware. To get on with the business of creation.

In 1965, in Holmdel, New Jersey, two radio astronomers named Arno Penzias and Robert Wilson set out to measure the radio waves emitted from our galaxy. By aiming the mechanical ear of a twenty-foot horn reflector of an ultra-low-noise radio telescope in different directions and comparing the noise they received with the virtually motionless noise of liquid helium, they would be able to determine source and filter out static. Expecting very little electrical noise, they began listening at relatively short wavelengths.

No matter where or when they listened, Penzias and Wilson kept picking up microwave radiation background noise equivalent to 3.5 degrees Kelvin. Everywhere in the universe, there was this hum. But it was only when cosmologists took seriously the implications of the "big bang" cosmogony that they realized what Penzias and Wilson had discovered. If the universe had begun from one point with this great bang, then as it expanded, its once equivalent temperature of billions upon billions upon billions of degrees would be lowered over the aeons to a predictable few degrees Kelvin. And it would appear naturally as background noise coming equally from all directions. This static, fossil-like radiation, then, was the most ancient signal ever received by astronomers.[8] None other than the ember-fading glow of the primeval fireball itself. A feeble, dwindling hum of the moment of creation.

The echo of one electromagnetic chord that is the sound of creation. It is soft. Perhaps the softest sound next to no sound there could be. But it can be heard. Heard by each generation. flickering toward us from long-since-fled galaxies. Through the air we breathe. A sound that seems to issue through the molecules of breathing bodies and inorganic matter. A kind of hovering in which we talk and imagine and see. Perhaps, in the medium of consciousness, the cosmic microwave radiation of creation's sound persists. But, because we have never heard its "silence" go off—just as we do not notice the refrigerator's hum until it stops—we do not know what it sounds like.

There is preserved in the rhythmic pulse of subatomic particles a faint sound of the very first moments. And if memory is some kind of record from which we can draw at will, then the universe hums with a kind of memory of its own genesis. And the sound of the Holy One of Being hovering over the face of the waters can still be heard even unto this very day.

THE SPECTRUM OF BEING

And it is then, from this hovering presence over the waters, that the One of Being says, "Let there be Light." And with the same simple mystery that thought becomes speech or that intention becomes action or that energy becomes matter: "There was Light." Not a second idea or the next step but all part of the flow of one sentence. (The divisions between phrases and words and letters are a human invention.) Here the "Let there be" and the "And there was" are both of one totality.

Consciousness alters the physical universe. The Newtonian, everyday, cause and effect, determinist, material world, which has room only for billiard balls and the laws that predict how they move, is violated by the Holy One of Being who speaks "Let there be" as well as by ordinary physicists who, by observing their experiments, alter the results. It is a "word" that does not cause but rather is synchronous with its creation: "And there was." At least in the beginning, thought, word, and consciousness are the same as thing, world, and creation. Materialism and idealism dissolve into one another. The work of the first day is not just "light," but the "and God spoke" that occurs at the same moment. And it is this consciousness and its creation that together give birth to day and night. Underlying the endurance of this world is the One who says, "Let there be Light," since beneath this world a consciousness-like-light glistens and ultimately, consciousness and matter are one.

In the late nineteenth century, James Clerk Maxwell integrated theories of electricity, magnetism, and light into one general formulation. Subsequent generations of scientists would discover and add such phenomena as radio waves and gamma rays to fill out the entire electromagnetic spectrum, until finally X-rays, radar, heat, radio waves, and visible light are now understood as bands of a larger whole. Differing in frequency and wavelength, but substantially the same. Einstein demonstrated that matter itself is yet only another form of energy, that the structure of space and time was itself connected to and curved by gravity. Here was the vision of a new kind of physics working toward a "unified field," in which all manifestations of reality are "scientifically" interrelated. And physicist John Archibald Wheeler, in his theory of geo-metrodynamics, has suggested that matter is actually a disturbance in the underlying structure of space-time.

Where do we fall on the spectrum? We have not yet been able to place the consciousness of the one who is arranging and observing the spectrum itself. The one who watches the unfolding of creation. The one who speaks and the experiment begins. And surely the One who spoke and being began.

Werner Heisenberg, one of the first generation of quantum physicists, discovered that "our acts of observation alter the states of the particles we observe."[9] According to what Heisenberg called the uncertainty principle, detached objective observation—on the most primary and subatomic level—was not possible. The very act of "observing" an event changes it. Observer becomes participant. All being, from space to time, matter to energy, intention to creation, is on one spectrum. Or, more correctly, they are different facets of the one underlying reality.

Matter is no longer matter but patterns of energy. Radiation, like light, is perhaps itself only a transient form of consciousness. In such a way, the consciousness of "let there be" can actually translate into "and there was." Consciousness fashions cosmos.

The mystery, then, is not so much that intention and word, mind and matter, space and time can "affect one another," but why we seem to perceive them as being discrete at all. The continuum of being extends through all the manifestations of being including human "beings." Our consciousness, that elusive, still unexplainable (apparent) dimension of ourselves, and perhaps (probably, unquestionably) our hallmark and "reason" for being is to matter and time as red is to blue and yellow. It is as simple as "And the One spoke"—and "there was." In the words of one of the most eloquent contemporary exponents of this "spectrum of being," William Irwin Thompson: "The universe is not a black box containing floating bits of junk left over from the big bang explosion; it is a consciousness saturated solution. Mind is not simply located in the human skull; animal, vegetable, and mineral forms are all alive."[10] Is this process called consciousness somehow fundamentally the same as what we also call light?

The first creation was light. It is, as the philosopher Ernst Cassirer has shown, a metaphor for consciousness raising itself from the dark oblivion of unconsciousness.[11] The One of Being brought forth consciousness from the primeval chaos of unawareness. Might this be true not only for the psychic history of the individual (ontogeny), as Cassirer's thoughtful reading of creation mythology teaches, but also as a literal insight into the origin of the universe itself (phylogeny)?

What we ordinarily call light is but a relatively narrow band of waves of radiation near the center of the electromagnetic spectrum. This phenomenon is doubtlessly due to the fact that most of the sun's radiation is also of the same frequency. Most life on earth has consequently evolved so as to make maximum use of it. But, of course, there is much more to light than meets the eye. Such electromagnetic energy, in its broadest sense, pulses within all being, possibly including consciousness itself. Light then might be more than just a metaphor for consciousness. And when Genesis "remembers" that the first utterance of the Holy One was, "Let there be light," it may know more than it lets on. (Dreams do, on occasion, partake of eternal truths.) This might also explain our fascination with this light-like-consciousness and our equal inability to comprehend it.

We seem condemned to (re)discover time after time that you cannot behold that of which you are made without ceasing to be who you are. Before people are born and after they die they "behold a great light." But not as long as they remain who they are. We are part of what we seek to study. Philo similarly has observed, "As in the case of light, which can only be seen by means of light, so too, God is not to be conceived except through Him: 'The questers after truth are they who envisage God by paeans of God, light by means of light.'"[12] "A photon, the ultimate unit of Light (consciousness), can be seen only once; its detection is its annihilation. Light is not seen; it is seeing."[13] This paradox is expressed in the description of the photon, the fundamental subatomic "particle" of all radiation. It is a particle without mass, neither a wave nor a thing. Nevertheless, packets or "quanta" of them make up the waves and the motions that seem to be the infrastructure of being. Are they not perhaps what is spoken of in the myth as the hidden Light of the first "days" of creation?

Here, in the consideration of light, the truth traditions of science and religion converge. It is a no-place of no quantification and no qualification. It is where mind and matter meet. The underlying river of consciousness itself. It is more than the ordinary light that illumines this page, which is nothing more than a gross metaphor. It is the light of consciousness that was hidden away after the first week of creation.

The Zohar too knows this, (I, 31b-32a) for it reminds us that this first-day light preceded the fourth-day creation of the sun. "The original light that God created...this is the light of the eye. It is the light that God showed to Adam, and through which he was able to see from one end of being to the other....Rabbi Isaac said...The light was hidden away in order that the wicked of the world might not enjoy it and it is treasured up for the righteous.... 'Light is sown for the righteous'"(Psalm 107:11). This Light is called the *or ganooz*, the light stored within.

This finds an analogue in recent cosmological theory. We understand that in the very early universe, above the temperature threshold of 4,000 degrees Kelvin, energy itself was not, as it is now, contained in the masses of atomic particles, but in the form of radiation.[14] There were then at least two distinct eras. The first era was dominated by radiation, pulsing electromagnetic waves of energy everywhere. "The roar of light." But as the winter chill of our present cosmos set in, the second era began. This one is dominated by gross matter. Material substance containing trapped light. We feel it in our bones. There is even a tradition in the Lurianic Kabbala that tells of holy sparks or *nitzotzot* imprisoned in everything and yearning to be set free through the agency of human intention and deed.[15]

Picture them for a moment. Transitory bits of light. Sparks. Present now and then they are gone. Left over from the creation event. Caught inside everything and everyone. A light-like consciousness. Echoing the beginning. Hovering just above at 3 degrees Kelvin. Somewhere between spirit and matter. Hidden in galaxies and trees and you and me. Shimmering. Like sunlight on water that will not be still. Set before us.

There is a legend of a second kind of Light. Saturday evening, after the withdrawal of the primordial Light (of consciousness) and the setting of the sun, Adam was left in utter darkness. It was then that he rubbed stones together and initiated fire: humanity's response to its own darkness and exile, its way of making it through the night. Fire is manmade consciousness: humanity's attempt to endure unredeemed creation. In much the same way that everything must pass through the nothingness on its way to becoming some thing else, so too is fire the symbol for material transformation. The chemical reaction through which the sacrifice becomes an offering and matter becomes energy. "Command the children of Israel to bring you the pure oil of beaten olives for lighting; to keep a light going continually." (Leviticus 24:2)

Controlling it is not only evidence of human uniqueness but also symbolizes organized religion. When the "light" was withdrawn, when we were left alone without the immediate awareness of the Holy One, we were able to make do with religion. This was a kind of stop-gap measure until the final reunification:

> "Rabbi Samuel bar Nahman said: In this world people walk in the light of the sun by day and the light of the moon by night, but in the time to come they will not walk by the light of the sun by day or the light of the moon by

night....And by whose light will they walk? By the light of the Holy One." (*Pesikta deRab Kahana, Kumi Uri,* 21)

It is as if the primary act of creation is to simply become conscious, and that through becoming conscious we—like God—create ourselves. The first and most important creation that human beings and the One of Being can give birth to is awareness. Eyes open, remade for wonder. Eyes that see. Ears that hear. Hands that feel. Breathless for a moment, we behold the dawn. The first light. An idea dawns. And what was nothing comes into being: Let there be Light.

Humanity, one might say, is the organ of consciousness in the universe. We are the result of consciousness's desire to become aware of itself. As Jung observed, "If the Creator were conscious of himself, he wouldn't have needed us."[16] Being speaks of and listens to itself through humanity. Our wickedness is creation's perversion. Our vision is creation's hope. If all existence is one organism, then humanity is its eyes and ears, its hands and its heart. The universe is sentient because we are part of the universe and we are sentient. Human awareness is as empirical and incontrovertible a fact as gravity or photosynthesis. Our amazement, our tears, our intuitions, and our silences are part of being. And for us to call the cosmos insensate would be like our eyes surveying our body and calling it blind.

Of course, there is no consciousness in the universe without humanity. Humanity is the organ of consciousness in the universe. And for this reason we hold our Creator hostage; without our eyes, the Holy One of Being would be blind. Insensate. Bumping into galaxies. Compelled to begin all over again. When we see, it is not only for ourselves. Another One sees through our seeing and stands behind us. A river of light flows within.

A consciousness-like-light wells up through and creates each order of being. Atomic particles. Atoms. Molecules. Minerals. Plants. Animals. Humanity. In an inexorable desire to become aware of itself, each of us carry these layers in our psyche, our genes. Go down through your layers and your childhood and your dreams. Through the apes and the amphibians and the fish and the protozoan slime. Through the volcanic waters and the carbon dioxide to the light-like-consciousness by which being began and by whose still, soft hum we are blessed to breathe and wonder. It is a spiritual ontogeny recapitulating a metaphysical phylogeny. The layers run back through time, but also all the way down to the source.

At the beginning of being, there is light: the light of the first day, the light that preceded the sun. And at the height of consciousness there is light: the light that is treasured away for the righteous ones. From this light, we emerge into the world and to it we return. Since all being emanated from it, we cannot "see" it. And therefore it "appears" as nonsense, or simply as nothing at all. Yet humanity, refusing to believe the evidence right before its eyes, stubbornly, in each generation, through the word of sacred myth or the hands of trusted technology, returns again and again to the spirit, to searching for the light.

When we return to creation thus, we reenter a mode of consciousness in which consciousness and its "object" are the same. But as we saw (and learned) at Sinai—to become conscious of our own consciousness is impossible, at least in our present evolutionary form. Our next shape and our final shape will be as beings of pure light, of pure consciousness. To become aware of the work of creation—go back through light that we see, to light that is more than we can see, to the soft pulsing echo of creation, to the nothing point of the origin/Genesis of all being. Then, we become nothing.

You Are Here

As a birthday present not long ago, I got a sailor's hand-held navigational computer. It's not much bigger than a pack of cigarettes. On only a few AA batteries, the gadget's antenna can pick up the signals of satellites orbiting the earth. Once it gets three clear signals, it makes a "fix" and, within half a football field's length of accuracy, you can know where you are anywhere on the surface of the earth. And then you'll know how to steer toward your destination. Well, sort of.

It turns out that knowing how to get somewhere requires a lot more than simply knowing your latitude and longitude coordinates. In addition, you must have a map or a chart and—here is the part we often forget—you also need to know where something *else* is on the map. It could be a lighthouse, the direction of North, or, for that matter, if you were looking at one of those information boards in a shopping mall, where another store is *in relation to* where you are standing. You might say that there's more to getting somewhere than simply knowing where you are. Orientation also requires some *other* fixed point. I was a crew member on a boat sailing up Lake Michigan through the night when I learned this.

At such a time, there is only you, the other members of the crew and the boat, patiently working her way through the waves and the night. Deprived of light, the effects of wind and waves can only be felt. The sea seems bigger than in the daylight. After a while, you get confused about where you end and the boat begins and where the boat ends and the water begins.

Ahead of you in the evening lies the last thin strip of twilight, a barely visible line of dark purple separating the upper waters from the lower waters. Then, without any sound of protest, it dissolves.

Gone. Now the only visible remains of the terrestrial world are in the distance behind: the slowly sinking, ten-second, white flash from the lighthouse on Point Betsy. That bright burst of light, higher than the horizon, will faithfully continue to provide a line of position. You may not know exactly how far away you are, but you do know, at least, that you are somewhere on that line.

As you sail farther and farther into the empty black, even Point Betsy misses a beat. Like a candle or a life going out, she flickers. Then she, too, is gone. Blackness everywhere. With her, you were oriented. Without her, you are not only alone in the dark, you cannot even be certain where you are.

Each lighthouse has its own distinctive pattern of flashes, a coded light-message that enables approaching mariners to identify their location on the chart. They are all recorded in *The Coast Pilot Light List*. They are all that any lighthouse ever says: "This is who I am. This is who I am. This is who I am."

Meditation before The Song of Songs

SO HERE I AM, O' One I am to love with all my heart,
Waiting to be damaged by love's selflessness
or destructive through its selfishness.
Where once there was fragrance
And melody and form,
Softness and sweet,
Now only glamour remains.
Let me trust again in love's naive ability
To restore my soul.
Let it be for me; for the one I love; for Your sake.
May the uniting of one lover with another
fashion a like union in the highest orders of Being,
Reuniting male and female dimensions
Of Your holiness.
The six days of creation
With the seventh day of *Shabbat*,
Sun with moon, daylight with night dark,
Insight with intuition,
Sending with receiving, having with being,
What can be told with what cannot, right with left.
Sides not only of Your holiness, but within myself.
Let me remember, One of Unity,
That all the ways of one in love
Are also the ways of Your Torah:
Affection and ecstasy,
Song and whisper,
Sharing, creating, being at once parent and child.
Surely, as it has been taught of old,

The day of the giving of the Song of Songs
Was the holiest day.
Holy One of Being, let me awaken
To the dew of my youth.
Let me be worthy to live again on the holiest day.
Let me belong to my beloved
And let my beloved belong to me.

I Believe in the Coming of the Messiah

Of all the seminal creative, mischievous, destructive, cockamamie ideas for the Jewish people to come up with and for Jews and other people to take literally, surely none could be more catastrophic than the idea of a Messiah. I mean, let's just make a list of really weird, dangerous religious ideas that are clustered around the Messiah.

That a person, a human being of flesh and blood, could come and resolve all pain and suffering, superimpose humane values on nature, so that we get, in poet Stephen Mitchell's words, "nonviolent wolves and vegetarian lions," reconcile every dispute and disagreement, turn the hearts of the parents to the children and the hearts of the children to the parents, convince all soldiers to beat their swords into plough shares and their spears into pruning hooks, give everyone his or her justly deserved reward or punishment. All of this is to be preceded by a cataclysm of literally cosmic proportions. And, oh yes, by the way, this person will also restore the Davidic monarchy, resurrect the dead, make Jews Masters of the Universe, and get everyone to make *aliyah*—moving back to Israel! We have here a fairly big idea.

But *that's* not amazing. What boggles the mind is that people buy the whole shebang. They give up all their earthly possessions, uproot their families, found new religions, and, generation after generation, gratefully even lay down their lives.

With the simple liturgical switch from *goael*, redeemer, to *geulah*, redemption, the early Reform radicals de-fused the Messiah time-bomb by redistributing the social burden among the membership of the entire community. They said, in effect, we are all the Messiah!

It occurs to me that this also has the unintentional side effect of cutting down on the number of messianic claimants. It's one thing to say you want to be the Messiah, but who in his or her right mind would claim to be an entire age?!

Perhaps we have been asking the wrong question. We are not strangers to reading sacred tradition as metaphor. Surely we understand that the sanctity of a text can be increased by reaching beneath its literal meaning. Maybe all this looking for the Lord's Anointed was never meant to be taken literally. Or, to ask it another way, "For *what* is the Messiah a metaphor?"

One clue may be the teaching that the Messiah will only come when things get so bad we cannot live without him [*sic*] or so good we don't need him. Indeed, we often say that all the contradictions, paradoxes, and antinomies will be resolved when the Messiah comes.

No wonder that, among Jews, the phrase "When the Messiah comes" means "Never!" That explains why the poor guy who was hired by the townspeople to wait for the Messiah at the outskirts of town consoled himself by saying that the pay is lousy but at least he had a lot of job security.

When the Messiah comes, light and dark, love and hate, male and female, being and nothing, even good and evil will at last be in perfect and Divine balance and we will understand how they all fit together and even why it seemed so important that they were once in conflict. But until that time, the syntax written in our brains cannot simultaneously comprehend a thing and its opposite.

Perhaps that is the metaphor: the resolution of all contradiction. You may say, just hold on a minute. If we admit tolerance for contradiction into our linear logic, we are going to have one big social mess on our hands. I agree with you. Consider as evidence the history of messianisms throughout human history. Claiming to abolish human suffering, they have all succeeded in making more.

Is it any wonder that after all these centuries, we Jews are so "Messiah shy."

Not everyone needs the Messiah with equal urgency. There are some personality types—let us call them left-brained or generically "masculine"—who focus on the otherness of evil in this world and the extreme transcendence of God from it. For them, faith is a mechanism for enduring life's excruciating contradictions, which can only be overcome finally by Divine super-imposition. Nachman of Bratslav said that when the Messiah comes, faith will become reason. Belief will be logical, linear, self-evident, obvious, and without contradiction.

If your logic is linear, if it sorts through one thing at a time, then your only way out is through an end to time. If, on the other hand, you are more right-brain dominant or generically "feminine," you may have noticed you have a high tolerance for paradox. Indeed, you often find it mysteriously beautiful. Evil often seems to be another dimension of the good, God seems to be present within all creation, and paradox is a natural way of comprehending existence. For such personalities, the idea of a Messiah is anti-climactic, unnecessary. Who needs a Messiah when your tolerance for paradox enables you to find God everywhere?

The problem is that we are all uneasy mixtures of both right and left. And, you should excuse the expression, only when the Messiah comes will we, and our world, be in balance.

Unless this yearning to transcend such paradox is itself just another example of the tyranny of the left cerebral hemisphere, with its uncompromising insistence on linear logic.

Perhaps the Messiah is nothing more than a projection of order's need for the absence of contradiction. Indeed, what if the other side of our brain, the right cerebral hemisphere, which loves paradox, were dominant? Then the idea of some future Messiah might not even have occurred. Within right-brain grammar, paradox is not only tolerated but cherished: Lions lie down with lambs, and lambs don't get much sleep. In fact the lions eat them, but that's what lions and lambs do to and for one another. The hearts of the children will be turned to the hearts of the parents for a while, and then they will fall back into screaming and fighting with each other because that is what parents and children do. Then, as the old time Reform Jews intuited, we won't need to return to Israel because Israel will be in us.

The way things are just now already can be messianic. And, if that is so, then the end of days is now and the Messiah is already here.

Rabbi Joshua ben Levi asked Elijah, "When will the Messiah come?" Elijah said, "Go and ask him yourself." Ben Levi found the "son of David" doing emergency medical intervention at the gates of Rome. He told Ben Levi that he will "come today." Ben Levi went back to Elijah and complained that he has been ripped off, for surely the Messiah is not coming today. But Elijah only explained that the "today" referred to Psalm 95:7, where we read, "Today, if you will listen to My voice." (*Sanhedrin* 98a) In other words, the Messiah will come only when Israel listens to the voice of God.

Listening to the voice of God means attaining a higher rung of awareness, one in which hearing God's voice is routine. When you can hear God's voice, then it's the Messianic Time. But if you can't, if you are still unable to comprehend paradox or endure the commonplace contradictions and the thousand natural shocks to which flesh is heir, then Moses and Elijah themselves could bring you sandwiches of honey-dipped *chalah* and leviathan and you'd order tuna fish instead.

Maybe my mother was a greater theologian than I realized. When she told me to become the Messiah, I thought she meant I should enter rabbinic school. I had no idea she meant that everyone of us already is. You are the Messiah. You already have everything you need, and you are where you need to be.

Epilogue

I HAVE WORN GLASSES SINCE I WAS FOUR YEARS OLD. That was back when glasses were made of glass and kids who wore them were called "four-eyes." They were a social embarrassment and a catastrophe for virtually all contact sports. I still wear glasses, and while I have given up football and my friends call me more imaginative nicknames, I wish I really had more than two eyes. That may be why I write: this process of trying to get thoughts into words seems to actually improve my vision.

Michael's Bar Mitzvah

THE RED CARPET IN THE SANCTUARY of our synagogue is laid directly over the cement of the foundation. That's what Michael's head hit when he went down: the cement. You could hear the crack. He didn't pass out. When people pass out they melt into a pool. They can be caught. Michael just took a half step backward, as if he were trying to give himself some distance from the Torah scroll and his own bar mitzvah. But instead he toppled straight back like a felled tree. When I turned around, I saw blood oozing from his left ear. I was certain he had fractured his skull, maybe worse. His mother screamed, "Oh God, not that! Not now!" (Not *what*? I wondered.) She used his new prayer shawl to try to stop the bleeding. "He has an infantile seizure disorder," she said. "He hasn't had one in over five years. We thought he was cured."

Michael lay there, unconscious.

We joke about the danger of holy moments: "The Great and Terrible Oz," *Raiders of the Lost Ark*, "Don't get too close to holy things or you might get zapped." Things like that. But we don't really believe them. At least most of us didn't until Michael's bar mitzvah. Now we're a little less cavalier. The congregation came together. People waited patiently in their seats. Physicians who were present came forward. The rescue squad arrived and took Michael to the hospital. Michael's mother, on her way out the door, asked us to please eat the luncheon lest it go to waste. I told the congregation that the doctors would do their job, Michael's family would do theirs, and that ours—even though none of us felt much like it—was to complete the service. Someone pointed out that we had forgotten to recite the concluding Torah blessing and respectfully suggested that the bar mitzvah might technically still be in progress. After the service, I waited around at the luncheon for a few minutes but had no appetite; my heart was at the hospital.

When I arrived in the emergency room, I found Michael encased in an orange spinal brace and wearing an oxygen mask. But now everyone was smiling. "The X-rays and CAT scan show no serious damage," his mother whispered. "The doctor says he'll be fine."

Michael was conscious—maybe more conscious than anyone else in the room. He looked up at me and proceeded to recite the three rules of checkers as taught by Rabbi Nahum, the son of the Rabbi of Rizhyn, which I tease all my bar mitzvah students they must memorize:

"You can't make two moves at once…You can only move forward and not backward…And once you reach the last row, you can move wherever you want."

Then he said, "Did I finish? Am I a bar mitzvah?"

"Oh, yes," I sighed. "You did the whole thing—and more."

ORIGINALLY PUBLISHED IN *MOMENT* MAGAZINE, 1992

Why I Am a Jew

IN THE TWILIGHT OF THE TWENTIETH CENTURY, with people trying on varying parts of and even *whole* religions like shoppers trying on clothing in a bargain basement, anyone who remains a Jew must be considered a "Jew by choice." Unfortunately, choosing one's way over another's risks chauvinism.

Chauvinism is a distorted love of self achieved through denigrating others just as self-hate is a distorted love of others achieved through denigrating oneself. They are both variations of the same primary insecurity. Being a Jew may be the right choice and, indeed, the only viable one for most Jews. But not because Judaism is better (or worse) than any other religion. Look at it this way:

Imagine a deck of fifty-two religious playing cards. Each one represents a different, primary religious idea, such as salvation, love of neighbor, God, afterlife, guilt, charity, revelation, and the like. Any decent religion must—in order to be a religion—play with a full deck. The difference between one religion and another is the "order of the cards," the "stack of the deck." In one spiritual tradition, the first card is "salvation," while "revelation" doesn't show up until card number forty-three. In another religion, the order may be reversed. What, we must ask ourselves, would be the top cards in the Jewish deck?

To hazard an answer, we must cut through centuries of apologetics. It was once fashionable, for example, to boast that Judaism gave the world ethical monotheism. The rarely challenged implication was that being the first to come up with an idea meant you owned it or excelled at it. Even worse, it implied that non-Jews were culturally or genetically inferior when it came to figuring out that there is a Holy Oneness to all Being or behaving ethically toward one another. Furthermore, if we are to include in our spectrum of Jews such diverse expressions as Ethiopian, Reform, Israeli, and Lubavitch, we cannot honestly speak of a singular or exclusive Jewish culture.

The following seem to me to be some of the "top cards" of the "Jewish deck," the core of the way we Jews have tried to make spiritual sense out of the mystery of life. They transcend geography and society. They have been with us since we bothered recording what was important. They keep appearing among Jews generation after generation. Apart from my birth, they are why I continue to be a Jew.

Not only does the God of the Jews have no image, but the God of the Jews has no personal history and no Name that can be spoken by human vocal cords. Indeed, the Name itself is made from the root letters of the Hebrew verb "to be" and probably means something like, "The One who brings into being all that is." With a God requiring so much imagination, Judaism is not likely to become one of the world's major religions in the near future. But there is more.

Somehow this "Source of all Being" can "get through" to human beings, or at least, anyone who is listening. The result of "getting through" is what we Jews call Torah. It is, you might say, a description from "The Source of All Being" of "The Way of All Being." Trying to understand Torah constitutes the highest activity of mind, just as living in accordance with it is the highest expression of human conduct. In the words of the proverb: "She is a tree of life to those who hold fast to her."

Now the content of the actual "revelation"—the one that legend says happened on Mount Sinai—was only that it is possible for the One of Being to "speak" with human beings. This same insight is echoed in another legend: Only the first letter of the first word of the first utterance was given. But that letter is *aleph*, the first letter of the alphabet and is customarily unpronounceable. But it does not have, as many think, no sound. To be precise, it is the sound the larynx makes as it clicks into gear; it is the mother of all articulate speech; it is the softest audible sound there is. Any other noise will drown it out. This was the same sound Elijah the prophet heard when he stood on the place where Moses stood and heard the *kol d'mama daka,* the thin, barely audible sound of almost breathing.

This quiet sound and the sustained, silent attention that renders it audible place demands on behavior. We Jews believe that such "commandments" are woven into the very warp and woof of creation. Each individual and each generation see them through unique lenses. But taken together, they describe how we understand our purpose as a people. And to ignore them is more than abdicating an existential responsibility: It is a sin. This routine and unfortunate alienation from the Source of our true selves can only be repaired through the act of *teshuva.*

Teshuva is the ever-present possibility, urge, and gesture of returning to our Source, the Holy One of All Being. Through *teshuva* all life is returned to its source. As Rabbi Abraham Isaac Kook, the great mystic, teaches, it flows unnoticed throughout creation. *Teshuva* is not simply apologizing or making right the damage we have done—though these surely are prerequisites. It is only this: The Return. *Teshuva* is the hardest thing in the world: To *fully* make *teshuva* would bring the Messiah. But it is also the easiest thing: It has only to *occur* to you to make *teshuva* and you've already begun.

More than just an individual gesture, *teshuva* is a great world-yearning that flows through and animates all creation. Through attempting to repair and heal what we have done in the past, we set it within a larger context of meaning and effectively rewrite the past. What was once only some thoughtless or even wicked act, now—when viewed from the perspective of our present *teshuva*—becomes only the embarrassing commencement of this greater healing now realized.

We stubbornly—and despite all the evidence—look forward to a time when all creation will join in the Great Return, a unity of all the world that will reflect the Unitary Source of all Creation.

ORIGINALLY PUBLISHED IN THE *JOURNAL OF REFORM JUDAISM*, 1978

A Teacher's Blessing: Berakhot 17a

MAY YOU LIVE TO SEE YOUR WORLD FULFILLED.
May your destiny be for worlds still to come,
And may you trust in generations past and yet to be.

May your heart be filled with intuition
and your words be filled with insight.
May songs of praise ever be upon your tongue
and your vision be on a straight path before you.
May your eyes shine with the light of holy words
and your face reflect the brightness of the heavens.
May your lips ever speak wisdom
and your fulfillment be in righteousness.

Even as you ever yearn to hear the words
of the Holy Ancient One of Old.

BY LAWRENCE KUSHNER

THE BOOK OF LETTERS: A MYSTICAL HEBREW ALEF-BAIT. New York: Harper & Row, 1975; Woodstock, Vt.: Jewish Lights Publishing, 1990.

THE BOOK OF MIRACLES: A YOUNG PERSON'S GUIDE TO JEWISH SPIRITUALITY. Special 10th Anniversary Edition: Woodstock, Vt.: Jewish Lights Publishing, 1997; softcover edition: New York: Union of American Hebrew Congregations, 1987.

THE BOOK OF WORDS: TALKING SPIRITUAL LIFE, LIVING SPIRITUAL TALK. Woodstock, Vt.: Jewish Lights Publishing, 1994.

GOD WAS IN THIS PLACE AND I, i DID NOT KNOW: FINDING SELF, SPIRITUALITY AND ULTIMATE MEANING. Woodstock, Vt.: Jewish Lights Publishing, 1991.

HONEY FROM THE ROCK: VISIONS OF JEWISH MYSTICAL RENEWAL, New York: Harper & Row, 1977; Woodstock, VT: Jewish Lights Publishing, 1990.

THE INVISIBLE CHARIOT: AN INTRODUCTION TO KABBALAH AND SPIRITUALITY FOR YOUNG ADULTS, with Deborah Kerdeman. Denver, Colo.: Alternatives in Religious Education, 1986.

INVISIBLE LINES OF CONNECTION: SACRED STORIES OF THE ORDINARY. Woodstock, Vt.: Jewish Lights Publishing, 1996.

THE RIVER OF LIGHT: SPIRITUALITY, JUDAISM AND THE EVOLUTION OF CONSCIOUSNESS. New York: Harper & Row and Rossel Books, 1981; Woodstock, Vt.: Jewish Lights Publishing, 1990.

SPARKS BENEATH THE SURFACE: A SPIRITUAL COMMENTARY ON THE TORAH, with Kerry Olitzky. Northvale, N.J.: Jason Aronson, 1993.

"A Hasidic-Spiritual Commentary," co-written with Nehemia Polen. In *My People's Prayer Book,* vols. 1 and 2, edited by Lawrence Hoffman. Woodstock, Vt.: Jewish Lights Publishing, 1997.

"Silencing the Inner Voices." In *Meditation from the Heart of Judaism,* edited by Avram Davis. Woodstock, Vt.: Jewish Lights Publishing, 1997.

"The Synagogue and Caring Community." In *Imagining the Jewish Future: Essays and Responses,* edited by David A. Teutsch. Albany: State University of New York Press, 1992.

"Ports of Entry: Introductory Texts on Judaism." In *A Reader's Guide To Jewish Books,* edited by Barry Holtz. New York: Schocken Books, 1991.

"The Unity That Is Not One," in *Ehad: The Many Meanings of God Is One,* edited by Eugene B. Borowitz. New York: *Sh'ma* Publications, 1988.

"Lawrence Kushner." In *Visions and Voices: Ten Conversations,* edited by Jonathan Cott. New York: Doubleday, 1987.

"Communities within Synagogues." In *The Jewish Catalogue III,* edited by Michael and Sharon Strassfeld. Philadelphia: Jewish Publication Society, 1980.

NOTES

NOTES TO SECTION 1 / *AMAZING GRACE*

[1] *Menahem Nahum of Chernobyl, Upright Practices, The Light of the Eyes*, trans. Arthur Green (New York: Paulist Press, 1982), 100.
[2] Martin Buber, *Tales of the Hasidim: The Early Masters*, trans. Olga Marx (New York: Schocken, 1947), 55.
[3] Harold Bloom, *Kabbala and Criticism* (New York: Continuum, 1983), 125.
[4] Aldous Huxley, *The Doors of Perception* (New York: Harper & Row, 1954), 22–23.
[5] Henry David Thoreau, *Walden and Other Writings*, ed. Brooks Atkinson (New York: Random House, 1937), 81.
[6] Eliyahu KiTov, *Sefer HaParshiyot* (Jerusalem: Aleph Publishers, 1965), *Parashat Terumah*, 128 (Hebrew).
[7] *Menahem Nahum of Chernobyl*, 100.
[8] *Itturay Torah*, ed. Aaron Greenberg (Tel Aviv: Yavneh, 1976), 6 vols. (Hebrew), vol. II, 248.
[9] *Itturay Torah*, vol. III, 199.

NOTES TO SECTION 2 / *WORDS OF FIRE*

[1] Johannes Pedersen, *Israel: Its Life and Culture*, vol. I (London: Oxford University Press, 1926), 135.
[2] Emil A. Gutheil, *The Handbook of Dream Analysis* (New York: Liveright, 1951), 550.
[3] Pedersen, 36.
[4] Norman O. Brown, *Life Against Death: The Psychoanalytic Meaning of History* (Middletown, Conn.: Wesleyan University Press, 1959), 320–321.
[5] Frederick S. Perls, "Dream Seminars," in *Gestalt Therapy Now*, ed. Joen Fagan and Irma Lee Shepherd (New York: Harper & Row, 1971), 212.
[6] Ira Progoff, "Waking Dream and Living Myth," in *Myths, Dreams and Religion*, ed. Joseph Campbell (New York: E. P. Dutton, 1970), 176–77 .

Notes to Section 3 / *Arguing with Heaven*

[1] David R. Blumenthal, *God at the Center: Meditations on Jewish Spirituality* (San Francisco: Harper & Row, 1987), 25.

[2] Aryeh Kaplan, *The Hasidic Masters and their Teachings* (New York: Maznaim Publishing, 1984), 21.

[3] The Midrash identifies him with Job's comforter of the same name. Louis Ginzberg, *The Legends of the Jews* (Philadelphia: Jewish Publication Society, 1909), vol. I, 421.

[4] *Itturay Torah*, vol. II, 304.

[5] Daniel C. Matt, "Hasidic Texts with Prefatory Note," *Studia Mystica* 10, no. 2 (summer 1987): 7.

[6] Alexander Altmann, "God and the Self in Jewish Mysticism," *Judaism* 3, no. 2, (1954): 146.

[7] Matt, "Hasidic Texts," 7.

Note to Section 4 / *Creation's Blueprint*

[1] Gershom Scholem, *Major Trends in Jewish Mysticism* (New York: Schocken, 1941) 283.

Note to Section 5 / *Acting Like the World Depends on It*

[1] Bradley Artson, "Rethinking Sexuality: Judaism and Homosexuality," *Tikkun* 3, no. 2 (March-April 1988): 52–54.

Notes to Section 6 / *A God Who Looks like Nothing*

[1] Richard L. Rubenstein, *Morality and Eros* (New York: McGraw-Hill, 1970), 186–87.

[2] Alan Watts, *The Book: On The Taboo Against Knowing Who You Are* (New York: Collier Books, 1966), 13.

[3] Arthur Green and Barry Holtz, *Your Word Is fire: The Hasidic Masters on Contemplative Prayer* (Woodstock, Vt.: Jewish Lights Publishing, 1993), 14.

[4] Gershom Scholem, *On the Kabbalah and Its Symbolism* (New York: Schocken, 1965), 30–31.

[5] Moses Maimonides, *Mishneh Torah, Hilkot Yesoday Torah*, 2.10.

[6] Nachman of Bratslav, *Likkutei Moharan* 21:11.

[7] Erich Neumann, *The Origins and History of Consciousness* (Princeton, N.J.: Princeton University Press, 1954), 6, quoting Ernst Cassirer.

[8] Rabbi Burt Jacobson, "The Glorious Presence: An Interpretation of the Teachings of Rabbi Israel Baal Shem Tov," 2nd draft (1978), 14.

[9] Mordecai HaKohen, *Al HaTorah* (Jerusalem, 1968), 489–90.

[10] Buber, *Tales of the Hasidim*, 174.

[11] Moshe Idel, *Kabbalah: New Perspectives* (New Haven: Yale University Press, 1988), 35.

[12] Ibid., 39 ff.

[13] Nachman of Bratslav, *Likkutei Moharan* 21:11.

NOTES TO SECTION 7 / *EYES REMADE FOR WONDER*

[1] Gershom Scholem, *Zohar: The Book of Splendor* (New York: Schocken, 1949), 27–28.

[2] Steven Weinberg, *The First Three Minutes: A Modern View of the Origin of the Universe* (New York: Bantam Books, 1979), 45.

[3] Ibid., 68.

[4] P. C. W. Davies, *Space and Time in the Modern Universe* (Cambridge: Cambridge University Press, 1977), 167–68.

[5] Weinberg, *Three Minutes*, 4.

[6] Davies, *Space and Time*, 120.

[7] Menahem M. Kasher, *Encyclopedia of Biblical Interpretation*, vol. I, trans. Harry Freedman (New York: American Biblical Encyclopedia Society, 1953), 5.

[8] Weinberg, *Three Minutes*, 45, 59.

[9] Ibid.

[10] William Irwin Thompson, *Darkness and Scattered Light: Speculation on the Future* (New York: Doubleday, Anchor, 1978), 138.

[11] Erich Neumann, *Origins and History*, 6.

[12] Ephriam E. Urbach, *The Sages: Their Concepts and Beliefs*, vol. II, trans. Israel Abrams (Jerusalem: Magnes Press, 1975), 781, note 21, 45–46.

[13] Arthur M. Young, *The Reflexive Universe: The Evolution of Consciousness* (San Francisco: Delacorte Press, 1976), 11.

[14] Weinberg, *Three Minutes*, 69–79.

[15] Scholem, *On the Kabbalah*, 125–26.

[16] Lyall Watson, *Lifetide: The Biology of the Unconscious* (New York: Bantam, 1980), 73.

This book and its jacket were designed by the author.
They were produced in Adobe PageMaker 6.5 and Illustrator 7.0.
The text face is Minion, designed by Robert Slimbach
and issued in digital form by Adobe Systems in 1989.
The display font is Marigold, designed by Robert Baker
and released by Agfa Compugraphic in 1989.
The Hebrew font, named Stam, was designed by the author and is
based on the scribal alphabet used in writing scrolls of the Torah.